MUSCLE & CHROME

Classic American Cars

Publications International, Ltd.

Louis Weber, CEO
Publications International, Ltd.
8140 Lehigh Avenue
Morton Grove, IL 60053

ISBN: 978-1-64030-384-3

Manufactured in China.

8 7 6 5 4 3 2 1

Credits

Photography:

The editors would like to thank the following people and organizations for supplying the photography that made this book possible. They are listed below, along with the page number(s) of their photos.

Ken Beebe: 76-77; Michael Brown: 38-39; Gary Greene: 80-81; Thomas Glatch: 106-107; Sam Griffith: 10-11, 36-37, 40-41, 50-51, 54-55, 60-61, 88-89; Jerry Heasley: 52-53, 116-117; John Heilig: 86-87; Don Heiny: 48-49; Bud Juneau: 14-15; Milton Kieft: 8-9; Bill Kilborn: 30-31; Dan Lyons: 6-7, 144; Vince Manocchi: 12-13, 16-17, 46-47, 58-59, 66-67, 94-95, 102-103, 122-123, 124-125, 126-127; Roger Mattingly: 92-93; Doug Mitchel: 22-23, 56-57, 70-71, 72-73, 100-101, 104-105, 108-109, 114-115, 118-119, 128-129, 130-131, 134-135, 138-139; Mike Mueller: 64-65, 90-91, 98-99, 142-143; David Newhardt: 82-83; Al Rogers: 24-25; Tom Salter: 136-137; Gary Smith: 62-63; Richard Spiegelman: 20-21, 34-35; Rich Szczcpanski: 68-69; David Temple: 18-19, 32-33, 42-43; Phil Toy: 28-29, 110-111; Andre Van De Putte: 120-121; Bill Watkins: 26-27; W.C. Waymack: 74-75; Nicky Wright: 112-113, 132-133, 140-141

Cover: Al Rogers

Owners:

Special thanks to the owners of the cars featured in this book for their cooperation.

Dennis P. Babcock: 81-81; Richard Bailey: 32-33; Alan N. Basile: 84-85; William Bauce: 72-73; Larry Bell: 112-113; Don and Carol Berg: 62-63; Jim Blanchard: 58-59; Ken Boorsma: 68-69; Rick Cain: 140-141; Jerry Capizzi: 54-55, 60-61; Robert N. Carlson: 8-9; June Cecil: 126-127; Jerry Charter: 44-45; Classic Auto Showplace: 136-137; Classic Car Centre: 132-133; Roger Clements: 38-39; Dr. Steven Colsen: 10-12; Richard J. Corsello: 100-101; Thomas and Mae Crockatt: 102-103; Dan Darling: 70-71; Wayne Davis Restoration: 52-53; Chuck and Sutton Decker: 74-75; Paul Eggerling: 40-41; Bill Ehrsam: 24-25; Paul E. Fadgen: 12-13; Eugene Fattore Jr.: 88-89; Gordon Fenner: 18-19; Bev Ferreira: 14-15; Ray Frazer: 26-27; Dr. Ernie Hendry: 30-31; Bill Henefelt: 64-65; David Hill: 20-21; Rich Hogbin: 124-125; Matt Lazich: 122-123; Garey Maib: 94-95; Mike and Marjie Markowski: 86-87; Brian R. McArthur: 106-107; Paul McGuire: 90-91; Glenn Moist: 120-121; Ronald S. Mroz: 92-93; MyHotCars.com: 110-111; Dick Nelson: 42-43; Alfred and Mary Ellen Oeding: 56-57; Norm Olsen: 104-105; Donald Passardi: 6-7; Andrew Peterson: 114-115; Donald Phillips: 138-139; Richard Presson: 36-37; Jim Reilly: 134-135; Michael Riebe: 48-49; RK Motors Charlotte: cover; David L. Robb: 98-99; Jeff Ruppert: 130-131; Joe Scariff: 28-29; Eugene Schild: 34-35; Tom Schlitter: 116-117; Gary Schneider: 108-109; Frank Spittle: 76-77; Allan St. Jacques: 82-83; Stephan M. Thomas: 50-51; Mike Venarde: 118-119; Volo Auto Museum: 128-129; Bob Ward: 22-23; George Watts: 46-47; John Willows: 16-17; Vince Zankich: 66-67

Table of Contents

Series: V-8		
Convertible		
Weight	**Price $**	**Production**
3340	1982	1209
Engine		
Type	V-8	
Displacement (ci.)	239.4	
Bore × stroke	3.19 × 3.75	
Horsepower	100	
Compression ratio	6.80:1	
Fuel feed	Holley 2-bbl	

Although a warmed-over continuation of the 1942 Fords with a revised hood and grille, the beautiful Sportsman convertible is the most coveted of the early-postwar Fords. Minuscule production of 1209 made the car a rarity even in its day.

Although an undeniably special automobile, to Ford executives the Sportsman was eminently "doable" because of the company's vast northern timber holdings, a processing plant at Iron Mountain, Michigan, and a decade of experience with manufacture of Ford woody wagons.

Sportsman's frame of solid wood blocks was assembled by hand over the steel skeleton of a modified stock convertible. For 1946 only, the framing was Ford's "A" style with full-length horizontal members. The 1947 and '48 cars employed "B" and "C" styles with vertical segments.

On bodysides and trunklid, maple or yellow birch framed mahogany inserts. A great deal of handwork was required to set and mitre the frame and decorative pieces, and buyers understood that the wood's hand-rubbed finish and structural integrity had to be carefully looked after.

Ford's 239.4-cid flathead V-8 mated to a three-speed manual produced 100 horsepower, which was sufficient to motivate the 3340-pound Sportsman with adequate pep.

Sportsman came standard with leather upholstery, hydraulic window lifts, and dual visor vanity mirrors. Despite being priced higher–$1982–than any other Ford to that time, Sportsman found more than 1200 buyers, a satisfactory number for a unique standard-bearer capable of pulling customers into Ford showrooms.

Another 2250 were produced for 1947 and just 28 for 1948 (the '48s were '47s with new serial numbers). After that, Ford pulled the plug.

The 1946-only Mercury Sportsman convertible was nearly identical, save for modest changes to the grille. The Merc was beautiful, too, but its $2209 price limited output to just 205 units.

The first '46 Ford Sportsman was delivered to Hollywood actress Ella Raines (*Phantom Lady; Hail the Conquering Hero*) on Christmas Day, 1945—just three months after Henry Ford II (Henry's grandson) assumed the presidency of Ford Motor Co. The mahogany for the prototype Sportsman (a car requested by Henry II) was the same as what the company used in its wartime construction of gliders. Given the expense of materials, generous standard features, and relatively low production, the $1982 '46 Sportsman was the first Ford since the 1908 Model K to flirt with two thousand dollars. In 2006, a restored '46 Sportsman sold at auction for $194,000, a healthy price warranted, in part, because the joins of the restored wood sections matched the technique of Ford's original workmanship.

Series: Town & Country		
4-door sedan		
Convertible coupe		
Weight	**Price $**	**Production**
3955	2713	2651
4332	2998	3136
Engine		
Type	inline-6	
	inline-8	
Displacement (ci.)	250.6	
	323.5	
Bore × stroke	3.44 × 4.50	
	3.25 × 4.88	
Horsepower	114	
	135	
Compression ratio	7.00:1	
	7.50:1	
Fuel feed	carburetor	
	carburetor	

For 1941–42, Chrysler's Town and Country cars had been steel-roofed, fastback luxury woodie wagons in the Royal and Saratoga/New Yorker series, but for postwar 1946, Town and Country became its own series. The wagon body style disappeared, and the T&C now was offered as four-door sedans, an inline-eight convertible coupe, and a pillarless coupe that stands as Detroit's first true hardtop. A two-door brougham was essentially a prototype, and production was limited to one. A six-cylinder convertible coupe, too, saw only one example, and seven prototype hardtops were built.

Town and Country's prewar luxury appointments returned—most noticeably the white ash bodyside framing and mahogany inserts. All T&Cs rode a 127-inch wheelbase that was a Saratoga/New Yorker holdover from 1942.

The 323.5-cid, 135-hp I-8 convertible was especially popular, which forced Chrysler engineers to come to grips with the related issues of no real roof support, and all that wood. In the end, a conventional floor section was used, with a surrounding steel beltline and rear fenders tied together by a steel shelf. Wood B-pillars were reinforced and linked across the floorpan via tunnels that connected to upright angle-iron supports.

The precisely made doors were essentially all wood, their considerable weight supported at the hinges by a sturdy sheet metal leading edge.

So complex was all of this that filing and welding of metal pieces had to be done by hand. Wood sub-assemblies on ragtops and steel tops alike were also handwork.

Only 10 Town and Country cars could be produced during the course of three eight-hour shifts. Just 5787 T&Cs were produced for 1947, with fully 3136 of those the ragtops.

Styling changes were minor through 1948—but the genuine mahogany inserts were replaced late in 1947 with Di-Noc decals.

The eight-cylinder sedan was gone for 1947, and the six-cylinder sedan was discontinued during calendar-year 1948.

Although 1946–48 Chryslers changed very little—the emphatic harmonica grille was a constant; likewise the cars' rounded, even bulbous lines—the '47 Town & Country was a head turner. Most were sold as convertibles and turned out to be more than competitive commercially with the Ford/Mercury Sportsman woodies, and with Nash's novel wood-bodied Suburban sedan. Wisely, Chrysler applied most of its resources to the Town & Country's wood bodies, though interiors had handsome wood insets and leather & Bedford cord upholstery. The T&C ragtop that returned as part of Chrysler's all-new 1949 lineup was a hardtop only for 1950 and, after that, a station wagon.

Series: Sixty-One		
Club coupe		
4-door sedan		
Series: Sixty-Two		
Club coupe		
Convertible coupe		
4-door sedan		
Series: Sixty Special		
4-door sedan		

Weight	Price $	Production
4068	2728	3521
4150	2833	5081
4125	2912	4764
4449	3442	5450
4179	2996	23,997
4356	3820	6561

Engine

Type	90° L-Head V-8
Displacement (ci.)	346.0
Bore × stroke	3.50 × 4.50
Horsepower	150
Compression ratio	7.25:1
Fuel feed	Carter or Stromberg 2-bbl

In a 2010 advertising campaign, GM's Cadillac Division resurrected a venerable slogan, with a twist: "The New Standard of the World." Cadillac was able to make a pretty good case for the claim in the new millennium, and it was hardly bragging when it introduced the slogan in 1948. After fielding warmed-over prewar designs for 1946–47, the marque burst forth with all-new styling for '48 that was highlighted by graceful rear-fender sweeps that culminated, strikingly, in tail fins.

The motif reflected the longtime fascination of designers Frank Hershey and Bill Mitchell with the configuration of Lockheed's fearsome and gorgeous twin-boom P-38 Lightning fighter-bomber. Mitchell was struck by a realization that, as he put it, "you could take one line and continue it from the cowl all the way back to the tip of the tail—that you could have one unbroken, flowing line."

Mitchell became occupied with other projects before the '48 Caddy was designed, but Hershey—who was named Cadillac design chief in 1944—maintained his enthusiasm for the Lightning's design cues. The Cadillac fins (which, at this stage, were actually more like pods) had no practical function but were nevertheless a sensation in the marketplace.

The fins brought a stately feel to the Sixty Special and Series Sixty-Two sedans and were downright rakish on the fastback Sixty-One club coupe Sedanet.

Model-year 1949 reiterated the fins and introduced a new model, the Coupe de Ville, to the Sixty-Two series. Along with the Olds Holiday and Buick Riviera, it was the first production hardtop on the American market.

The 1949 engine was new as well, an ohv V-8 that carried the mark of engineer Ed Cole, who would father the '55 Chevy small-block V-8. The '49 motor developed 10 more horsepower (160) than the aging L-head unit it replaced and offered a significant increase in torque: 312 pound-feet rather than the previous 274. The lighter '49 Caddys, such as the Sixty-One and Sixty-Two club coupes, were among the fastest cars on the road.

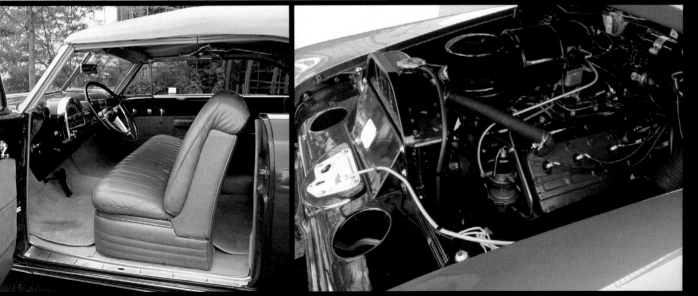

The upswept fins of the '48 Cadillac suggest aircraft design and have become justly famous for that, but aviation cues also are apparent in the wrapped front glass and handsomely curved dash with a rainbow-shaped "drum" that houses gauges and controls. Some basics of the car's body shape were fiddled with during the war (when no new automobiles were produced by Detroit). At war's end, the Caddy's design was developed further, and refined, at Franklin Hershey's small farm in suburban Detroit. By necessity, aircraft have outthrust noses that suggest aggressiveness; Hershey reflected that in the prowlike form of his Cadillac's hood near the nose, and with large eggcrate shapes in the grille.

Series: Commander

Regal DeLuxe 2-door sedan

Regal DeLuxe 5-passenger coupe

Regal DeLuxe convertible coupe

Weight	Price $	Production
3175	2046	85,839 (total)
3165	2072	
3385	2431	

Engine

Type	inline-6
Displacement (ci.)	226
Bore × stroke	3.31 × 4.38
Horsepower	94
Compression ratio	6.50:1
Fuel feed	Carter 1-bbl

tudebaker touted itself as "First by far with a postwar car!" when it chose early 1946 to announce its stylish, all-new 1947 Champions and uplevel Commanders (priced at $1661 to $2236). Head-turning design was the big attraction for '47 and, as here, for '48: nearly flush rear fenders, flow-through front fenders, and a low hood and deck. These changes already were in the cards throughout the industry, but the fact is that Studebaker had them on the road first.

Studebaker combined design elements created by Bob Bourke for Raymond Loewy Associates, Virgil Exner (created when he was with Loewy, and after he had left), and modeler Frank Ahlroth. Although Studebaker was by this time disenchanted with Loewy, the car's wrapped backlight and general shape came from that studio, via Bourke, with portions—notably the hood—by Exner.

Stude beat the Big Three to the new-design punch because the company's war-production plants made very limited use of machines and tooling that were needed for auto production. Simply put, Studebaker was able to get to work on new designs when the plants of other, larger manufacturers needed considerable time to retool for civilian production.

With the exception of the Land Cruiser four-door sedan, which rode a 123-inch wheelbase, Commander utilized a 119-inch span and was available as two- and four-door sedans, three- and five-passenger coupes, and as a convertible coupe.

Studebaker's sound financial condition meant that the company had the means to develop new engines, but because time was the tyrant, Stude carried on with its familiar 94-horsepower 169.6-cid L-head six.

Inside, instruments were grouped squarely in front of the driver, on a no-glare "black light" fascia that been developed for wartime use.

For 1947, Commander production was 56,399—about half the volume of the less-expensive Champion line. Commander production leapt to 85,839 for 1948 before dropping to 43,719 for 1949.

The '48 Studebaker Commander was based on the all-new body that had cost Stude $11 million to develop, and that had been introduced for 1947. Designer Bob Bourke had done preliminary sketches as early as 1940. For model-year 1948, Studebaker stood pat with its styling, earning more than $19 million on car/truck sales that were 85 percent higher than for the previous year. The company built more than 250,000 vehicles for the 1948 calendar year. Across the board, prices were hiked about $200. Postwar inflation accounted for most of this (Stude's materials cost more than before), but the automaker still moved up to seventh on the industry's production list for '48.

4-door sedan

Weight	Price $	Production
4200	4000	50

Engine

Type	flat 6
Displacement (ci.)	335
Bore × stroke	4.50 × 3.50
Horsepower	166
Compression ratio	7.00:1
Fuel feed	carburetor

reston Tucker was an innately appealing combination of salesman, visionary, and entrepreneur. He gained industry experience at Studebaker and Dodge, built Indy racers in the mid-Thirties, and built high-speed military scout cars a bit later in that decade. Restless and unabashedly grandiose, Tucker promised to build an automobile that would put the Big Three products to shame.

Naturally, he would name the car after himself.

Fifty hand-built Tuckers and one non-running mule were made. All were four-door sedans distinguished by boldness and innovation. The rear-mounted, water-cooled 335-cid flat-six was based on a military-helicopter engine; it produced 166 horsepower and an incredible 372 pound-feet of torque. The initial "Tuckermatic" transmission was inadequate and was ultimately replaced by a Cord unit.

The roomy, six-passenger cabin had a Hudson-style dropped floorpan that greatly increased interior room, and front and rear seats were interchangeable, to even out upholstery wear. Doors were cut up into the roof for easier entry and exit. A centrally mounted "Cyclops" third headlight turned with the front wheels.

Safety features included windshield glass that popped out harmlessly on impact, instruments and controls tucked beneath a padded dash, and an intriguing "Safety Chamber" into which front passengers could dive "in case of impending collision."

The car rode a 128-inch wheelbase and had a sturdy box-section perimeter chassis with a subframe at each end and all-independent suspension. Although it weighed a hefty 4200 pounds, the Tucker sprinted from zero to 60 mph in about 10 seconds.

Alex Tremulis's body design was dramatically aerodynamic, with sculpted front fenders; fastback roof; boat-tail deck; upright, high-mount taillamps; and latticed grillework front and rear.

The car died after Preston Tucker was indicted and tried for fraud related to the stock issue that funded the whole project. Acquitted, he still had the money needed to build the car but declined because public confidence had been fatally undermined.

Part of the appeal of the short-lived Tucker was that it reminded war-weary Americans of the futuristic automobiles and other elements of daily life that had been promised in magazines from *LIFE* to *Mechanix Illustrated* since the purposely predictive 1939 World's Fair. Torpedolike and aerodynamic, the Tucker was at once unorthodox and excitingly practical—something, in other words, to warm the hearts of futurists of all ages. The car stood just 60 inches tall—low for the day—and its adapted helicopter engine had a fully sealed water-cooling system, an industry first. The all-alloy engine weighed just 320 pounds at a time when a Ford flathead eight came in at 569 pounds.

Series: 70		
Hardtop coupe		
Convertible coupe		
2-door sedanet		

Weight	Price $	Production
4420	3203	4343
4370	3150	8244
4115	2618	18,537

Engine

Type	inline-8
Displacement (ci.)	320.2
Bore × stroke	3.44 × 4.31
Horsepower	150
Compression ratio	6.90:1
Fuel feed	Carter carburetor

The first Roadmaster arrived for 1936, coinciding with a linewide Buick redesign and the division's reworked and more powerful straight eight. A major restyle appeared for 1937, and then Buick stood pat until the line was extensively restyled for what turned out to be the war-shortened 1942 model year.

Much excitement was generated during model-year 1948 by the introduction of Buick's Dynaflow, the industry's first passenger-car torque-converter transmission. Initially on the options list, Dynaflow was standard on Roadmaster for 1949. That year also brought another restyle, which cut three inches from Roadmaster's wheelbase, bringing it to 126 inches. Overall length was cut, as well.

Roadmaster offered a sedan, fastback Sedanet, convertible, and Estate Wagon for 1949, plus (at midyear) a rakish hardtop coupe called Riviera.

Significant style innovations appeared this year. A slab-sided body ahead of the rear fenders brought Roadmaster in line with the even more revolutionary '49 Ford. Some Roadmasters had heavy chrome sweepspears that curved down and back before kicking up at the rear wheelwells.

Another '49 design innovation became a Buick signature: front-fender VentiPorts, popularly known as "portholes," were suggested by designer Ned Nickles. The VentiPorts on cars produced during the first part of the '49 run actually cooled the engine but were subsequently plugged and became mere decoration.

The inline eight that powered the '49 Roadmaster displaced 320 cubic inches and developed 144 horsepower, or 150 with Dynaflow. The car weighed more than two tons. Prices started at $2618, and production came to 87,019—sufficient to account for an impressive 26.8% of all Buick production for the year.

The 1949 Roadmasters had marshmallow-soft suspensions that encouraged wallow during cornering, and the cars were sluggish off the line, partly because the Dynaflow was prone to slippage (some critics dubbed it "Dynaslush").

But because the '49 Roadmasters were big, heavy cars with style that suggested affluence, they had many fans and remain highly regarded.

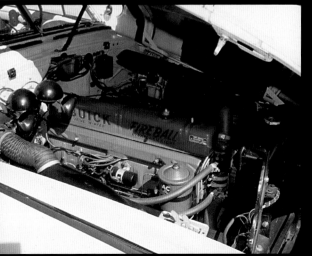

Buick was given completely fresh styling shortly before World War II, so the "old" design of the 1946-48 Buicks still seemed new and sales were strong. The 1949 Buick received new postwar styling that helped increase sales by more than 100,000 units. The eight-cylinder engines that propelled the Super and Roadmaster convertibles were noted for their smoothness. When that selling point was mated to the all-new Dynaflow transmission (a $244 option available on Roadmaster only), buyer response was so great that Buick had to double its projected number of Dynaflow units.

Series: Custom V-8		
Tudor sedan		
Club coupe		
Convertible coupe		

Weight	Price $	Production
2968	1511	433,316
2948	1511	150,254
3254	1886	51,133

Engine

Type	V-8
Displacement (ci.)	239.4
Bore × stroke	3.19 × 3.75
Horsepower	100
Compression ratio	6.80:1
Fuel feed	Holley 2-bbl

Ford sales for 1946–48 had been healthy—more than 429,000 units for 1947 alone—but the cars were moving because of Ford's enormous dealer network, and the public's postwar hunger for anything new, even facelifts of Ford's bulbous 1942 design.

Organizational redundancies left by the late Henry Ford were bleeding the company of cash, and independents the likes of Hudson, Studebaker, and Kaiser had taken the immediate-postwar design lead.

The slab-sided '49 Ford was the result of a design competition mounted by company president Henry Ford II, who knew that the postwar seller's market wouldn't last much longer. In-house staff and outside designers were invited to pitch ideas. Indie designer George Walker brought in Richard Caleal (a veteran of GM and the Raymond Loewy design house), Joe Oros, and Elwood Engel. When Caleal became disenchanted with the group's direction, he left to labor independently at his home in Indiana. Set up in his kitchen with clay modelers Joe Thompson and John Lutz, Caleal perfected his design.

Henry Ford II and other company execs viewed proposals created by Caleal, Ford styling chief E. T. "Bob" Gregorie, and Oros and Engel. The Caleal car was chosen, and it went into production virtually unchanged, save for a flip of the taillights from vertical to horizontal, with fairings that integrated them into the rear quarters. The new car made its GM and Chrysler rivals look old.

Ford enjoyed its best sales in nearly 20 years: more than 1.1 million units produced during the extra-long model year. Lower and lighter than the '48s, the '49 had a modern ladder-type frame with Ford's first fully independent front suspension. Its 239.4-cid, 100-horse flathead V-8 lent itself to aftermarket hop-up, and noise and handling problems that came with the rush to production were addressed as the design carried though for 1950 and '51.

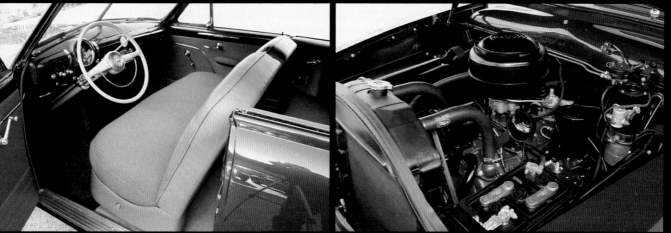

When Ford introduced a V-8 for model-year 1932, it gave itself an advantage over Chevy that endured until 1955. Ford's popular midsize flathead V-8 (239.4-cid) saw changes for truck use in 1948, and for the car line a year later. A new "Load-A-Matic" distributor was driven through a shaft mounted at a vertical right angle to the engine's axis. The studs and nuts that had affixed the head to the block were replaced by 24 bolts, and the bell housing was now cast separately from the cylinder block, and became a bolt-on item.

Series: Sport		
Roadster		

Weight	Price $	Production
2300	5500	fewer than 50

Engine	
Type	V-8 (Ford)
	inline-6 (Studebaker)
Displacement (ci.)	239
	226
Bore × stroke	3.19 × 3.75
	3.31 × 4.38
Horsepower	105
	94
Compression ratio	6.75:1
	6.50:1
Fuel feed	Holley 2-bbl
	Carter carburetor

Frank Kurtis was a chassis designer who began to build highly competitive dirt-track midgets and other racers in the Twenties. He later owned and campaigned Indy cars, winning the "500" four times between 1950 and 1955. But before those triumphs, Kurtis applied his expertise to a streetable sports car.

The '48 Kurtis Sport was a compact two-seat convertible on a 100-inch wheelbase. Tidily slab-sided, the Kurtis was only 169 inches in total length, and 68 inches across. Unusual for its day, the car employed unitized body/chassis construction. Ten panels comprised the body, all but two of them aluminum; hood and deck were fiberglass. The car was wrapped with a full-perimeter protective rub rail.

The Kurtis could be fitted with whichever engine a buyer wished to install, but typical examples ran with Ford's 239-cid flathead V-8, with Edelbrock manifolds, developing 100 horsepower. (Kurtis had run flatheads in some of his earlier competition cars and retained his fondness for them.) A Studebaker inline six of 226 cid, with 94 horsepower, was also available.

Power with the six wasn't extraordinary, but because the Kurtis weighed just 2300 pounds, the V-8 gave pretty good giddyap.

Specially tuned spring and damper rates brought stability and nimbleness.

True to the nature of European sports cars, the Kurtis had clumsy, clip-in Plexiglas windows. Things were easier upstairs, where a removable rigid top was included with the soft top.

Do-it-yourselfers could purchase a kit version that ranged in price from $1495 to $3495, depending on level of completeness. A "turnkey" Kurtis Sport cost $5500.

In 1950, Kurtis sold his tooling to L.A. auto dealer Earl "Madman" Muntz, who stretched the chassis to create the four-place Muntz Jet of 1951–54.

Frank Kurtis was a metalwork and body-design prodigy who supervised seven men by the time he was 17 years old. On his own later, in the Thirties and Forties, he designed and built midgets and other racers. Because he wanted to keep his crews busy during the off-seasons, he came up with a street car, the Kurtis Sport. The KS was available as a kit, in partially completed forms, and as a drive-it-away turnkey. Most engines were sourced from Studebaker and Ford, though many owners chose others. Standard running gear, including suspension and brakes, were off-the-shelf Ford parts. Test-trial success brought good publicity, including the cover of the first issue of *Motor Trend*. The Kurtis on these pages runs with Caddy's 331 that arrived for '49.

Series: 9CM		
Coupe		
Sport sedan		
Convertible coupe		
2-door wagon		
Weight	**Price $**	**Production**
3321	1979	120,616
3386	2031	55,882
3591	2410	16,765
3626	2716	8044
Engine		
Type	V-8	
Displacement (ci.)	255.4	
Bore × stroke	3.19 × 4.00	
Horsepower	110	
Compression ratio	6.80:1	
Fuel feed	Holley 2-bbl	

Ford Motor Company organized Lincoln-Mercury Division in 1947 as an answer to General Motors's stratified and highly profitable multi-division setup. For model-years 1947 and 1948, Mercs were virtually identical and typically postwar, with bulbous, old-style design and tall bodies. For model-year 1949, though, Ford-division design leapt ahead of GM and Chrysler with an all-new slab-sided beauty that helped ensure Ford's fortunes in the decade to come. Mercury, too, got fresh sheet metal that it shared not with Ford cars but with Lincoln.

Although not as revolutionary in its styling as the Ford (for instance, the Mercury still had suggestions of separate front fenders), Merc design was sleek and torpedolike, with a single bright molding that ran full length at mid-flank, and narrow glass all around. In that, and in its "inverted bathtub" shape, it was in the same camp as contemporaneous Hudsons and Packards.

As before, a single series offered four body styles: coupe, four-door Sport Sedan (with rear-hinged "suicide" back doors), a convertible, and a new two-door wagon.

Like Ford, the '49 Mercury was treated to a new chassis with fully independent front suspension, weight-saving Hotchkiss drive (that replaced torque-tube), and a live axle on modern parallel longitudinal leaf springs.

Mercury once again out-muscled Ford with a stroked 255.4-cid V-8 that used a Holley carburetor and 110 horsepower to become an off-the-floor 100-mph car for the first time. A $97 automatic overdrive option was teamed with a 4.27:1 rear axle instead of the more familiar 3.90:1.

With Lincoln styling, reasonable prices ($1979–$2716), and that powerful V-8, more than 201,000 '49 Mercurys found homes. That was more than three times the volume of Merc's previous best year and good for sixth place in the industry, another all-time high.

The darkly aggressive looks of the '49 Mercury attracted customizers almost immediately, particularly in Southern California, where the custom-car culture first took root. The graceful sweep of the back window and deck, and the car's narrow glass, got customizers thinking along sinister lines, and soon, lowered "bathtub" Mercs with chopped tops; cruiser skirts; and customized bumpers, headlights, and tail lamps were prowling local strips in cities and towns. The massive, clean bodysides were cleaned up even more, with removal of side chrome, badging, and even door handles. And in *Rebel Without a Cause*, actor James Dean piloted a mildly customized Mercury, thus stamping it on the collective consciousness of an entire generation.

Club coupe

Deluxe club coupe

Convertible coupe

Holiday hardtop coupe

Deluxe Holiday hardtop coupe

Weight	Price $	Production
3435	1878	10,684
3455	1956	10,772
3745	2294	9127
3510	2162	1366
3565	2267	11,316

Engine

Type	V-8
Displacement (ci.)	303.7
Bore × stroke	3.75 × 3.44
Horsepower	135
Compression ratio	7.25:1
Fuel feed	carburetor

Fresh postwar styling that germinated at Olds during 1946 came to fruition for 1948. Simultaneously, Olds engineers began work on a new, high-compression eight that broke from the existing L-head design. Tests with a high-compression (12:1) inline six that gave good performance and mileage led to a new, 90-degree Olds V-8 that the division initially designated the "8–90" or—in honor of former GM engineering guru Charles Kettering—"the Kettering." But the name that came later, and which still excites Olds fans decades after the fact, is "Rocket."

With bore and stroke of 3.75 × 3.44, the Rocket displaced 303.7 cubic inches. The motor developed 135 horsepower, and although its primary purpose was improved fuel economy for the reasonably heavy Olds 98, division engineer Harold Metzel (later Olds GM) pushed for the motor to be installed in the smaller, lighter 88 platform. (The 98's wheelbase was 125 inches; the 88's, a trim 119.5.)

The Olds 88 appeared in February '49, quite late in the model year, but accounted for more than 99,000 units of total 1949 Olds production of 288,310.

Eighty-Eight, as well as the junior 76 series, ran with the new Hydra-Matic self-shifter and shared GM's new 1949 A-body with Pontiac and Chevy but had a uniquely tweaked suspension with four-wheel coil springs, lever shocks, and anti-roll bars front and rear. Two massive stabilizer bars helped locate the rear axle.

The "Futuramic 88" lineup offered a full complement of body syles, but speed demons latched onto the 88 club coupe. The car was 300 pounds lighter than a comparable 98 and was a natural for stock-car racing: stable and, with manual (added for 1950), good for 12 seconds in the 0-to-60 run. Top speed in test runs was 96.9 mph.

Model-year '50 also brought designer Harley Earl's gorgeous pillarless hardtop coupe (exclusive to the 98 for 1949), a high point of early-postwar GM design.

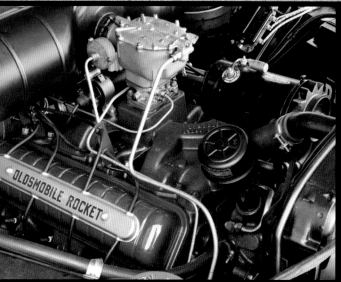

Partly because the nation's economy had settled down by 1949–50, by which time most of the immediate-postwar labor strikes had found resolution, many Americans wanted cars that were more than mere transportation. The '50 Olds 88 fit the bill because it borrowed the high-compression "Rocket" V-8 from the larger 98 series with the shorter, lighter platform of the make's six-cylinder cars. The 88's power-to-weight ratio was thus an impressive 25.5:1—sufficient to make the car one of America's first "factory hot rods." Performance and smart good looks, particularly in convertible form, were key to the 88's appeal.

Series: Manhattan		
4-door sedan		
Weight	Price $	Production
3771	3075	283

Engine	
Type	inline-6
Displacement (ci.)	226.2
Bore × stroke	3.31 × 4.38
Horsepower	115
Compression ratio	7.30:1
Fuel feed	Carter 2-bbl

Kaiser-Frazer Corporation was a partnership between shipbuilding magnate Henry J. Kaiser and auto-marketing genius Joseph Frazer. Production of new cars had been suspended across America during 1942–45, and Kaiser-Frazer anticipated the postwar seller's market.

And the K-F product wouldn't be the warmed-over 1942 models fielded by the Big Three, either, but all-new cars with modern features and clean, flush-fender styling by Howard "Dutch" Darrin.

Production began in June 1946 on two marques introduced as 1947 models: the medium-price Kaiser and luxury Frazer.

For Manhattan's first season, Frazer offered the nameless "Standard" and the uplevel Manhattan. Both were sedans riding a 123.5-inch wheelbase. They also shared a long-stroke 226.6-cid flathead six engine dubbed the "Supersonic Six." But with only 100 or 112 horsepower to push more than 3300 pounds of Frazer, the engine's main virtue was economy.

Except for a high, blunt hood, the Darrin body was sober but modern. Fenders sat flush against the bodysides, and the grille and chrome trim were restrained. Windshields were of the familiar two-piece variety.

The industry's widest front seat–64 inches–contributed to exceptional passenger room, and underneath, a rugged box-section chassis had a modern front-coil/rear-leaf suspension.

Manhattan sales dipped by half for 1948 (to 18,591, from the prior year's 32,655). After that, sales fell so dramatically that Frazer announced 1949–50 Manhattan sales as a single sum: 10,020.

The '51 Manhattans were essentially the1949-50 cars with revised styling. With money nearly gone, designer Herb Weissinger managed an effective but frankly cosmetic front and rear re-do.

K-F dealers liked the change, but only 283 Manhattans were produced.

On a brighter note, the 226.6-cid flathead six gained a few horses, to 115; compression ratio was improved, as well.

Of the total 1951 Manhattan run, a mere 131 were convertible sedans. Kaiser carried on into the 1955 model year, but Frazer was no more.

The postwar seller's market hung on during model-year 1948, but while other automakers continued to profit, Kaiser-Frazer struggled. Because K-F's capital was drying up, only a cosmetic re-do was possible for 1951, with the mandate that designer Herb Weissinger make good use of leftover, lower-level 1949–50 Kaiser bodyshells to field another season of upscale Frazers. K-F dealers liked the '51 Frazer's handsome new look and ordered 55,000 units. Unfortunately, K-F could produce only 10,214. Exit Frazer.

Series: 70		
Convertible coupe		

Weight	Price $	Production
4315	5000	1690

Engine	
Type	V-8
Displacement (ci.)	322.0
Bore × stroke	4.00 × 3.20
Horsepower	188
Compression ratio	8.50:1
Fuel feed	2-bbl carburetor

Buick said that Skylark was intended to capture the attitude of a European sports car. Well, that was puffery and nonsense because Buick knew it would never build a car that gave up any of the heft and luxury that captivated upwardly mobile Buick drivers. So Skylark (available only as a convertible) was big: 4315 pounds for 1953, stretching 207.6 inches on a 121.5-inch wheelbase. And at a boggling $5000, it cost 40 percent more than other Buicks. If 1953 hadn't been Buick's 50th anniversary, Skylark would probably never have been born at all.

Skylark began as the XP-300, a low-slung Motorama show car inspired by Buick designer Ned Nickles' custom treatment of his own '51 Buick. The XP-300 excited public interest and coincided with Buick's new, oversquare 322-cubic-inch, 188-horse V-8—the largest-bore Buick engine in 25 years.

Come that 50th birthday, and Skylark got the green light and the 322. The Dynaflow automatic was tweaked linewide for '53, retaining its smoothness while addressing sluggishness with new twin turbines in the torque converter. According to Buick, Twin-Turbine Dynaflow boosted torque by 10 percent and reduced engine rpm for quieter performance.

The Skylark's visual appeal remains startling. Division engineers and designers took the standard Century/Special body and chopped the windshield three inches and dramatically lowered the beltline. Seatbacks that sat level with the door tops added to what was essentially an illusion of pavement-scraping lowness.

To achieve cleaner-looking bodysides, Skylark dispensed with Buick's familiar VentiPort portholes. Forty-spoke chrome wire wheels were custom-made in Michigan by Kelsey-Hayes.

Skylark picked up 12 additional horses and a dramatically wrapped Panoramic windshield for '54, plus enlarged wheel openings and an emphatic rear deck topped by emphatically chromed taillight fins.

Always intended as a limited-run car, Skylark managed production of just 1690 units for '53 and a minuscule 836 for '54.

浩氣塞天金光遍地

五聖宮

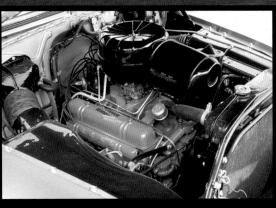

During the early Fifties, Buick's reputation for quality and sophistication were enviably good, bu smart automakers never rest on their laurels. The '53 Skylark, then, was a purposeful ste into the future: a beautiful, well-engineered car that would serve as Buick's flagship, boos the marque's reputation, and lure potential buyers into Buick showrooms. Buick genera manager Ivan Wiles was a great champion of the Skylark, which was given the go-ahead even though Buick fully expected to sell very few. As things unfolded, Skylark production hit 1690 units—better than, say, the 670 Roadmaster four-door wagons that were produced for '53 but significantly short of the 4282 Special convertible coupes, 6701 Super ragtops, and 3318 standard Roadmaster convertible coupes made that year. But what does immortality care about production figures?

Series: 290		
Convertible roadster		
Weight	**Price $**	**Production**
2705	3513	300

Engine

Type	inline-6
Displacement (ci.)	235.5
Bore × stroke	3.56 × 3.94
Horsepower	150
Compression ratio	8.00:1
Fuel feed	3 Carter 1-bbl

During 1951–52, GM design chief Harley Earl envisioned a two-seat sporty car that could be sold for about $1850, the price of a new Chevy sedan. With practical and morale-boosting support from new Chevy chief engineer Ed Cole, Earl sold top GM management on a fiberglass-bodied roadster that would alter Chevy's rather staid image. The subsequent 1953 Motorama show car called Corvette morphed, without significant alteration, into the production '53 Corvette.

Corvette was sleek and low. Unfortunately, a big reason for Chevy's staid image was its lack of a truly hot engine. Although Cole's team was at work on a V-8, Corvette's first engine (1953–55) had to be based on Chevy's 235.5-cid "Blue Flame" inline six. Producing just 108 or 115 hp in base and uprated form, respectively, the motor was tweaked with triple carbs, solid valve lifters, and a higher-lift camshaft. All of that, plus an improved compression ratio of 8.0:1 (from 7.5:1) brought output to 150 hp (155 for 1954–55).

Although no beast (0–60 mph in 11 seconds), the pumped-up six was nevertheless too much for Chevy's manual transmission, so all '53 'Vettes had a two-speed Powerglide automatic.

A new X-member chassis was strong, but the suspension was basically the same as what Chevy had been using since 1949, albeit with revised shock rates.

As manufacture began, GM became concerned about the fiberglass, which mandated slow, careful assembly that limited production to 50 cars a month. Total Corvette production for '53 was 300. Even at $3250 retail, all 300 were pre-sold.

The first Corvette was widely praised for its low center of gravity and stability in the twisties—hallmarks of European sports cars that didn't emphasize acceleration anyway.

The following year, about 1500 '54 Corvettes remained unsold, and the car was perilously close to being canceled. It wasn't, of course—but that's a story for later in this book.

More than 65 years on, the '53 Corvette remains startlingly handsome and appealing. Although in some details very much a car of its era (rocket-pod taillights, an anemic inline six), the first 'Vette was laudably understated in its general body shape and trim, and suggested a relaxed affluence as clearly as it promised top-down freedom. And with its fiberglass body, it was adventurous and predictive. It wasn't very fast, but its fans say that it didn't really have to be.

Series: Hardtop Dragon		
4-door sedan		
Weight	Price $	Production
3320	3924	1277
Engine		
Type	inline-6	
Displacement (ci.)	226.2	
Bore × stroke	3.31 × 4.38	
Horsepower	118	
Compression ratio	7.30:1	
Fuel feed	Carter 2-bbl	

The first Dragons were trim options available with Kaiser's Traveler series for 1950–51, and with a few Manhattans for 1952, when the Dragon option wasn't officially offered. But for 1953, Dragon became a discrete series and carried on with the remarkable and very pleasing array of interior fabrics (by Carleton Spencer), rolled and pleated upholstery, fabric-covered roofs, and two-tone bodies. If all that was insufficient to set these cars apart from the common herd, there was the hood ornament plated in 14-carat gold.

Spencer's use of textured "Bambu" vinyl created intriguing patterns in a variety of colors, with complementary seat inserts in knobby, faux bouclé vinyl designed by *fashionista* Marie Nichols. Carpeting was a special filament shag called "Calpoint," which also was used on the '54 Kaiser Darrin sports car.

The 3320-pound Dragon was powered by Kaiser's unspectacular 226.2-cid inline six developing 118 horsepower for 1953, up from 115. Top speed was a modest 90 mph, but 60 came up from rest in 15.0 seconds–not bad for the day.

Included among the standard equipment were four-speed Hydra-Matic transmission, radio, heater, carpeted trunk, and extra sound insulation. Power steering became available late in the production run.

At $3924, a Kaiser hardtop Dragon (not a true hardtop, as it had a B-pillar), cost just $17 less than a Cadillac Coupe de Ville. The Dragon was a shapely, very beautiful car (an evolution of designer "Dutch" Darrin's "Anatomic" styling of 1951), but because it lacked Cadillac's cachet and dealer network, only 1277 were produced. (By way of contrast, 14,550 Coupe de Villes were produced for '53.)

Dragon was an agreeable long-haul touring car, but the power steering was twitchy and, underneath all the glamour, it was just another competent six-cylinder sedan. But if style earns points, Dragon gets extra credit.

Although to some eyes eccentric, the '53 Kaiser Dragon is arguably among the most beautiful American cars of the Fifties. Mechanically competent and unusually well finished, it captures the uplevel make at a late high point. For the first time, consumers were introduced to cars with unusual fabrics, colors, and textures. Design specialist Carleton Spencer was among the very few in the auto business who stopped to consider what women might like to see in a car. The results of his study matched up closely with one done by *House and Garden* magazine, so Spencer worked closely with the publication as he developed his patterns, colors, and textures. Twenty years later he said, "We didn't have a bunch of different engines...to make cars different....We had only one basic body....Color and trim was where we had to achieve a difference."

Series: 2631

Convertible coupe

Weight	Price $	Production
4105	5210	750

Engine

Type	inline-8
Displacement (ci.)	327
Bore × stroke	3.50 × 4.25
Horsepower	180
Compression ratio	8.00:1
Fuel feed	4-bbl carburetor

I n-house Packard designer Dick Teague had been taken with the Pan American, a Packard show car and he was especially enamored of the low beltline created for the car by Richard Arbib. Teague wanted a similar beltline, but because the money wasn't forthcoming, he had to base his Caribbean design on the tall, "Contour-styled" Packards that had debuted for 1951. These were handsome automobiles, but their stance worked against the sporting nature Teague wanted to create.

He was given permission, however, to pick up some obvious—and relatively inexpensive—Pan American cues, including a broad hood scoop instead of the traditional chrome hood ornament, wire wheels in dramatically open wells, a flowing deck, and a "Continental" spare.

Mitchell-Bentley of Ionia, Michigan, received standard 1953 convertible bodies and customized them to Caribbean specs. The finished cars retailed for $5210—at a time when the average new American house cost about $9550.

The Caribbean was created as a deliberate counter to Cadillac's limited-edition Eldorado. The Caribbean cost $2500 less, and, indeed, it outsold the Eldo for 1953: 750 units to 532. But then came 1954 and a dramatic Cadillac restyle that lifted Eldorado production to 2150—a figure achieved, in part, by a $2000 price reduction on Eldo, which put it at $400 less than a comparable Caribbean. In the face of GM's great flexibility on price, Caribbean managed just 400 units for '54.

A Ford-GM price war put a big squeeze on independent automakers in 1954, so the Packard line mostly stood pat for 1954, postponing a redesign and a new, long-awaited V-8.

Packard's 327-cid, 180-horsepower inline eight powered the '53 Caribbean. For '54, the engine was upgraded to Packard's new 359 I-8, rated at 212 hp.

Two-tone paint appeared for '54. The rear wheel wells were squared off, and the grille and bumper were made less massive.

A second Caribbean generation, with a V-8, was rolled out for 1955–56, but it did even less well in the marketplace than its predecessor.

Packard may have wanted to release a limited edition "sports car" for 1953, but tight corporate money and market realities demanded that the Caribbean be a six-passenger cruiser based on standard 1953 convertible bodies, made sporty by cosmetic changes at wheel wells, hood, and deck. Given these strictures, designer Dick Teague—who was known around Packard as the "wizard of facelifts"—was both inventive and reasonably subtle, and first-year sales were good enough to offer some hope for Packard. Luxury leather interior trim and optional self-shift Ultramatic transmission helped move Caribbeans off dealer lots.

Series: Champion		
Regal Starliner hardtop coupe		
Series: Commander		
Regal Starliner hardtop coupe		
Weight	**Price $**	**Production**
2760	2116	13,058 (total)
3120	2374	
Engine		
Type	inline-6	
	V-8	
Displacement (ci.)	169.6	
	232.6	
Bore × stroke	3.00 × 4.00	
	3.38 × 3.25	
Horsepower	85	
	120	
Compression ratio	7.00:1 (manual)	
	7.50:1 (automatic)	
	7.00:1	
Fuel feed	Carter	
	Stromberg	

Raymond Loewy was an influential designer and an even better self-promoter, salesman, and judge of talent. Without his outsized presence it's possible that the '53 Studebaker Starliner hardtop—designed chiefly by Loewy associate Bob Bourke—might never have happened.

Bourke had a fondness for the Lockheed Constellation airliner, particularly the unified line that began at the tail and elevated modestly along the fuselage before making a subtle dip at the nose. Bourke saw purity of design in that and brought a similar sensibility to the Starliner's sweeping "character line" that ran back along the bodyside before bending down to the rocker panel in a reverse angle that duplicated the slope of the back fenders.

For the day, the Starliner was remarkably understated. An elongated, twin-nostril front grille and wrapped bumper were mirrored in upright tail lamps that appeared integrated with the rear fenders. The back bumper, too, though nicely shaped and subtly outthrust beneath each taillight, was understated and pleasingly integrated with the fenders and downsloped trunklid.

Because Studebaker wanted to differentiate itself from the Big Three, the Bourke-Loewy proposal was accepted, giving the make a chic, European air that was excitingly unique.

In entry-level Champion trim, the Starliner had an inadequate 169.6-cid inline six producing just 85 horsepower. The Commander version, though, ran with Studebaker's hardy 232.6-cid, 120-hp V-8, which produced a 100-mph top speed and zero-to-60 runs as quick as 13.0 seconds.

The pillared-coupe version of Starliner was called Starlight; together, they became known as "the Loewy coupes." Studebaker anticipated one Champion or Commander coupe being produced for every four sedans, but the ratio worked out to be the opposite. People wanted the two-doors, but because of problems that slowed production and encouraged short cuts and poor build quality that wasn't sorted out until the similar '54s, Stude lost customers faster than it gained them.

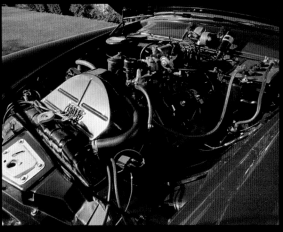

Anyone who wishes to make a point about organic design can hardly do better than to gesture in the direction of Studebaker's 1953 Starliner coupe. No styling element appears contrived or slapped on. Rather, the car looks like a living creature with features that evolved until the perfect symmetry of form and function was achieved. Further, the Stude was a modern-looking car at a time when GM and Chrysler automobiles were upright and bulbous. The Starliner's pleasing grille shapes were compromised a bit for 1954, when vertical "teeth" were added, but the look was still smart and, for the day, restrained. On the other hand, build quality of the '53s was indifferent, and the cars were alarmingly rust-prone. Brakes were merely okay. Stude addressed the problems for '54 but lost customers, even as it created a car for the ages.

Series: Monterey		
Monterey Sun Valley hardtop coupe		
Weight	**Price $**	**Production**
3535	2582	9761
Engine		
Type	V-8	
Displacement (ci.)	256	
Bore × stroke	3.62 × 3.10	
Horsepower	161	
Compression ratio	7.50:1	
Fuel feed	Holley 4-bbl	

Sun Valley was Merc's variant of the Ford Skyliner/Fairlane Crown Victoria, with a tinted Plexiglas front roof section and a deluxe interior—plus a useful clip-in sunshade for relief on hot days. And like the '54 Skyliner, the Sun Valley was a true pillarless hardtop. All of that amounted to legitimate novelty value, but the Sun Valley was essentially the same as Mercury division's steel-top hardtops.

A top-line model, the Sun Valley was available with Monterey in 1954 and with Montclair for '55. (In Canada, Sun Valley was part of the Monarch line.) Handsomely styled, it was a tweaked version of the 1952 design, but with a more emphatic grille, wraparound taillights, cowled headlamps, and additional bodyside chrome. The Plexiglas dome was its most noticeable feature, of course. Fans called it the "bubbletop." The less charitable referred to it as "the sweatbox" because air conditioning had to be purchased as an option.

The overhead-valve V-8 was nicely sized, displacing 256 cubic inches for 1954 and 292 for '55. Horsepower was 161 and 198, which meant satisfying standing-start performance; a low 3.90 rear axle and manual transmission helped. For 1955, the front suspension was upgraded to ball-and-socket, and all Mercurys got their first wraparound windshield.

Sun Valley production for model-year 1954 came to 9761 units, and 1787 for '55. Mercury ranked seventh in 1955 auto production, improving from about 260,000 units for 1954 to just under 330,000— a strong showing for a division that to some people was hardly different from Ford.

Despite the far greater number of 1954 Sun Valleys, it's the one that remains preferred by collectors, and is often seen with distinctive yellow paint that contrasts well with the dark green Plexi top.

Although Ford carried the Plexiglas Crown Vicky into 1956, the Sun Valley run concluded with the '55.

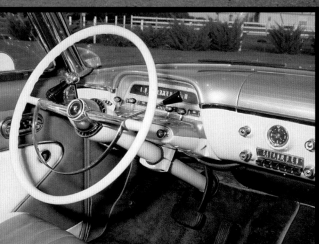

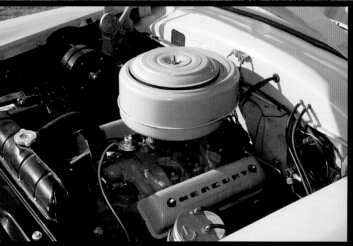

Advertising has always been given to excess, so it's impressive that much of this ad copy for the '54 Mercury Sun Valley rings true: "The heart of a city at night gleams with its own stars of neon and marquee. This is a magnificent sight....All the richness and color reaches you. Yet the intensity is softened, filtered by the tint of the plastic roof....You stop for a traffic light. You glance up through the top at the overhead signal. It turns green and you continue your pleasant journey—completely, wonderfully at ease." The Plexiglas top was tinted green to reduce interior heat, but the fact that *everything* would have a greenish cast wasn't mentioned.

Series: Bel Air		
Convertible coupe		
Hardtop coupe		
2-door Nomad wagon		
Weight	**Price $**	**Production**
3300	2206	41,292
3180	2067	185,562
3285	2472	8396
Engine		
Type	V-8	
Displacement (ci.)	265	
Bore × stroke	3.75 × 3.00	
Horsepower	162 / 180	
Compression ratio	7.50:1	
Fuel feed	Rochester 2-bbl	
	Rochester 4-bbl	

By the fall of 1954, Chevrolet had been the best-selling automobile in America for 19 consecutive years. Industry analysts figured that one of every four cars on the road was a Chevy. It's nearly impossible to mount meaningful arguments against that kind of success, but here's one: Ford cleaned Chevy's clock with its all-new slab-sided 1949 redesign, and Ford's V-8 engines, which stretched back to 1932, made Chevy's venerable inline sixes seem a little, well, leisurely.

There were reasons why Bonnie and Clyde favored Fords.

Because of visionary thinking done by GM design head Harley Earl and Chevrolet chief engineer Ed Cole, all of that changed with the '55 Chevy line. It was as if history had been tossed out the window. You noticed these cars.

Where the '54 Chevys had been upright, rounded, and faintly bulbous, the '55s were sleek, slab-sided, and aggressive: Ferrari-style eggcrate grille; subtly hooded headlights; dramatic "Sweep-Sight" wraparound windshield; a lowered beltline; rakishly backswept rooflines; and ornamental "hood bird." That was Earl and his team.

Inside were a twin-cowl instrument panel and better ergonomics all around, particularly a gearshift lever more conveniently sited than before.

And under the hood, a V-8 at last—and a fine one, too: a small-block unit displacing 265 cubic inches and rated at 180 horsepower—55 hp better than the top inline six of 1954. Compact cylinder dimensions and free breathing were critical to the engine's success. The motor was the work of Cole, who collaborated with Harry Barr and Edward H. Kelley.

The '55 Chevy was available in six Bel Air Series body styles, most memorably as the convertible, pillarless sport coupe and Nomad wagon. The Two-Ten Series offered six body styles; the One-Fifty, four.

Total 1955 Chevy car production was 1,703,993. That was good enough to extend its winning streak to 20 years: Ford's 1955 cars (themselves pretty spectacular) fell short at 1,451,157 units.

The basic 1955 body would see two more seasons, including the iconic '57, but the '55 remains the purest and most historically important.

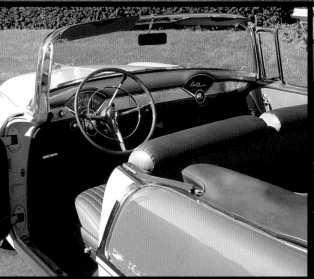

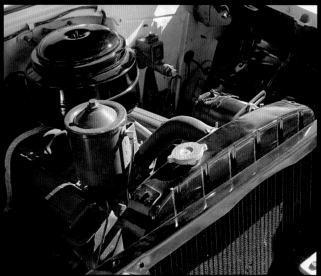

Ford jumped way out in front in the styling stakes in 1949, when its gorgeous, slab-sided, V-8-powered Tudor and Fordor sedans, and club coupes and convertibles, steamed up the inside windows of dealers across the nation. Chevy soldiered on with a venerable but outdated inline six—and then came the '55s, and it was like starting over. Not only did the '55 Chevys offer a capable V-8 that made Chevy fans cheer, the engine was beneath the hood of a stunningly smart, understated, slab-sided body. Elements intended to catch the eye were many: a Ferrari-like eggcrate grille, subtly hooded headlamps, slightly squared-off wheel openings, a lovely dip and kickup just aft of the coupe's doors, and a pleasing suggestion of fins. Improved road manners were in the mix, too, helping propel the '55 Chevy into a kind of instant folklore that's no less dramatic today.

Series: 300		
Hardtop coupe		
Weight	**Price $**	**Production**
4005	4110	1725
Engine		
Type	Hemi V-8	
Displacement (ci.)	331.1	
Bore × stroke	3.81 × 3.36	
Horsepower	300	
Compression ratio	8.50:1	
Fuel feed	two 4-bbl carburetor	

As late as model-year 1954, Chrysler products were tall and faintly dumpy, with hoods and rear quarters that bulged up and out from the body. For 1955, however, onetime Raymond Loewy associate Virgil Exner came up with a remarkable, thoroughly modern linewide redesign, which brought sleek slab sides and dramatically lowered greenhouses. In an allusion to the development expense borne by the corporation, the '55s Chryslers were touted as having "The 100-Million-Dollar Look."

A new, performance-oriented Chrysler was called the C-300. It combined a New Yorker hardtop body; Windsor rear quarter panels; and Imperial grille, front bumper, and parking lights. Wheels were Kelsey-Hayes wires. The division parts met a requirement laid down by Chrysler Division general manager Ed Quinn that the car's looks be in step with the rest of the line.

Chrysler Division's chief engineer, Bob Rodger, was a veteran of the Hemi engine project, and he gave the C-300 a stiffened suspension and a 331.1-cid Hemi V-8 developing 300 hp—hence the model name, and the highest power rating ever offered in a production car to that time. Sixty mph came up from rest in about 10 seconds, and top speed was an impressive 130 mph.

First-year C-300s were rather Spartan: leather upholstery and Powerflite automatic were standard, but many buyers restricted their options to radio, heater, and power steering. Air conditioning was not available.

At $4110, the C-300 was not only a corporate "super stock" but a very expensive one, too. Production for 1955 was 1725, and 1102 for 1956, when the $4419 300B ran with a bored-out 354 Hemi rated at 340 and 355 horsepower. A/C and a "Highway Hi-Fi" record player joined the options list for '56.

As had been hoped, the C-300 won big in NASCAR and AAA events in 1955 and '56, establishing credibility that has kept the Chrysler "letter series" cars collectible to the present day.

The '55 C-300 was a luxury car, but unlike others of the breed, the Chrysler didn't coddle its riders with marshmallow-soft road manners. To the contrary, the C-300 was as much a performance car as a luxury choice. It was no coincidence that this car, with the heavy-duty leaf suspensions, was named for its coupe body style and for the horsepower output of its brilliant Hemi engine. Although based on the New Yorker hardtop, the C-300 stood 1.5 inches lower than that car. It also had a speedometer calibrated to 150 mph—a bit optimistic, granted, but a suggestion nevertheless that this automobile wasn't designed for the timid. On the track, Tim Flock and Lee Petty piloted C-300s to NASCAR glory.

Series: Fairlane

Crown Victoria hardtop coupe

Weight	Price $	Production
3321	2272	1999

Engine

Type	V-8
Displacement (ci.)	292
Bore × stroke	3.75 × 3.30
Horsepower	198
Compression ratio	8.10:1
Fuel feed	Holley 2-bbl

Throughout the 1950s, Ford's big cars made just one arguable misstep, the ungainly '58. Other than that, the division produced one handsome, capable cruiser after another, beginning with the 1949–51 generation and progressing to the lower and wider 1952–54 models. It was this generation that defined what would be the "Ford look" for more than ten years, with rounded tail lamps, subtly squared wheel arches, squared-up rear deck, and a high, straight-through beltline.

For 1955, chief designer Frank Hershey introduced a wraparound windshield, full-width concave grille, modestly finned rear fenders, hooded headlamps, and interesting "speed lines" around the wheel arches. Front parking lights were larger and thrust outward from discrete pods.

The previous top dog, Crestline, was replaced by Fairlane, which included a Sunliner convertible, a Victoria hardtop, and a stylish Crown Victoria coupe that was offered with a Plexiglas roof panel or a full-steel roof.

All '55 Fairlanes had dramatic chrome spears that began on the inner edges of the headlight cowls and moved aft along the bodysides, to dip dramatically at the A-pillars before rising again to continue parallel to the long, crisp rear fenders.

The Crown Vic was particularly distinctive with its unique chrome "basket handle" that wrapped over the roof and fell in wide, graceful backslant above the door handles. When the transparent roof panel was ordered, the basket handle divided the Plexiglas portion of the roof from the steel. Because the basket handle added little or no structural strength, the Crown Victoria rode on a sturdy X-member frame of Ford's big convertibles—an idea of chief engineer Harold Youngren. Top motor for 1955 was a 198-horse 292 V-8.

For 1956, the parking lights became rectangular, and the distinctive bodyside chrome picked up horizontal ribbing. The 292 continued, now rated at 200 hp, but the max engine was a new 312-cid V-8 producing 215/225 horsepower.

For many years, the 1955–56 Ford Crown Victoria was neglected in collector circles because considerable attention was given to its main rival, Chevrolet. But where the '55 Chevy was a complete break with that marque's past, the '55 Ford was a natural but frankly exciting evolution of Ford's handsome 1952–54 generation. At once aggressive and stalwart, decorative but tasteful, the 1955 Crown Vicky is one of the prettiest cars of the period—and one of the most solid, too: Engineer Harold T. Youngren noted the hardtop's body flex and compensated by ordering the Sunliner convertible's stiffer X-member frame. This made the '55 and '56 Victorias unusually tight. The 292-cid V-8 was hearty, and just for fun, there was the available "Continental" spare, which gave this impressive car added presence.

Series: Thunderbird

Convertible with removable fiberglass top

Weight	Price $	Production
2980	2944	16,155

Engine

Type	V-8
Displacement (ci.)	292
Bore × stroke	3.75 × 3.30
Horsepower	192 (manual)
	198 (Ford-O-Matic)
Compression ratio	8.10:1 (manual)
	8.50:1 (Ford-O-Matic)
Fuel feed	Holley 4-bbl

The 1955 Thunderbird is one reason Chevy's Corvette avoided cancellation in its earliest years. Simply put, Chevy couldn't allow its roadster to be shown up by Ford's sporty V-8 T-bird.

And Ford knew it could not resist the challenge presented by Corvette's 1953 debut. Although legend holds that the 'Bird was conceived when Ford execs admired British and Anglo American sports cars at the 1951 Paris Auto Show, Ford had had a two-seat concept in the works for some time. Corvette appeared in January 1953. Ford, with preliminary work already complete, was determinedly hard at work just a month later on what would become the Thunderbird.

The T-bird had a traditional steel body, roll-up windows, and a power top or lift-off hardtop. In top trim, the 'Bird's 292-cid V-8 developed 198 hp, a figure that would rise to 202 hp for 1956, the year that brought a 312 V-8 rated at 225 hp.

For 1957, the last year of the first Thunderbird generation, the 292 was rated at 212 horsepower, the 312 at 300/340 (supercharged). Maximum Corvette horsepower for 1955 (its first year with a V-8) was 195, from 265 cubic inches. By '57, the top Corvette powerplant, a 283-cid V-8, produced 283 horses in top trim—57 fewer than Thunderbird.

Though snug on a 102-inch wheelbase (the same measure as Corvette's, by the way), Thunderbird was obviously a Ford, with rakishly hooded headlamps, straight-through rear fenders with discreet fins, a wrapped windshield, and round tail lights.

The efforts of engineer Bill Burnett and young designer Bill Boyer paid off enormously, as first-year 'Bird production was 16,155—enough to outsell the '55 Corvette by a margin of nearly 24 to 1. Production leveled to 15,631 for 1956, and then surged to 21,380 for 1957. Thunderbird had struck like lightning.

Chevrolet's Corvette appeared for the 1953 model year and initially struggled to win buyers—as well as fans at Chevy corporate. On the precipice of cancellation, Corvette was given a reprieve when Ford's V-8, two-seat Thunderbird appeared for 1955. Suddenly, 'Vette had a rival of sorts and a challenge that could not go unanswered. Corvette would live to see its clock cleaned by Thunderbird's performance and sales figures. Indeed, the 1955–57 T-bird generation was every bit as stylish as the Corvette, and much more an obvious member of the Ford family than Chevy's sports car was to its stablemates. The 'Bird had a continuity of division style that made it a more logical purchase than its competitor. Thunderbird was exotic yet reassuringly familiar, too. On every level, it was a great triumph.

Series: Imperial

Newport hardtop coupe
4-door sedan

Series: Crown Imperial

4-door sedan
Limousine

Weight	Price $	Production
4490	4720	3418
4565	4483	7840
5180	6973	45
5230	7095	127

Engine

Type	Hemi V-8
Displacement (ci.)	331.1
Bore × stroke	3.81 × 3.63
Horsepower	250
Compression ratio	8.50:1
Fuel feed	Carter 4-bbl

Chrysler made Imperial a distinct make for 1955. By that time, the Imperial name had been around for nearly 30 years, as the high-line Chrysler. Although "Chrysler" suggested style and engineering innovation, the Imperial wasn't in the same class as Cadillac or Lincoln or even then-floundering Packard, which was still hanging on in '55.

By making Imperial a separate line, the company not only took direct aim at Detroit's other luxury makes but announced that, like Ford and GM, it was going to build and sustain a multi-division corporation.

Chrysler cars were all-new for 1955, and Imperial was especially distinctive, with startling (yet understated) gunsight taillamps, a modestly wrapped windshield, wrapped backlight, a bold yet tasteful divided egg-crate grille, and circular rear-wheel openings.

The design evolved from the K-310 show car of 1951 and Virgil Exner's Parade Phaeton concepts of a year later. The Imperial's subdued side treatment and grille came from the Phaetons; the unique taillights were lifted from the K-310.

Imperial's 130-inch wheelbase was a few inches longer than that of contemporary Lincolns and considerably longer than Packard's.

Two volume models were offered: a two-door Newport hardtop and a four-door sedan. Additionally, a Crown Imperial riding a 149.5-inch wheelbase was produced but was unable to break the Caddy and Lincoln stranglehold on limo sales.

Although a convertible Imperial was mocked up, it did not enter production.

Chrysler's existing 331-cid "Firepower" Hemi V-8 was tweaked with a redesigned four-barrel carburetor and higher compression, for 250 horsepower, an impressive 15-hp bump over the engine's 1954 output. Powerflite automatic transmission was standard.

For 1956, very modest tail fins were added, and a Hemi enlarged to 354 cubic inches produced 280 horsepower.

Imperial continued without interruption through 1975. Many are striking and imposing; but the 1955–56 models are among the most coveted.

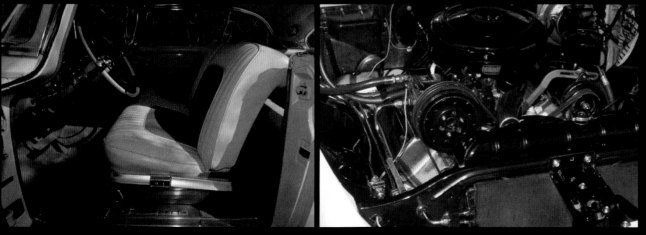

Imperial was offered in two wheelbases for 1955: the C-69 short-wheelbase Newport coupe (130 inches) and the C-70 Crown Imperial sedan (149.5 inches). The 331.1-cid Hemi V-8 had hydraulic valve lifters and an overhead-valve setup. The motor had a cast-iron block and five main bearings, and ran with a compression ratio of 8.50:1. A 4-barrel Carter carburetor fed gas into the engine's vacuum. Two forward gears were provided by a Torque Flite automatic. The engine wasn't tuned to have the muscularity of its C-300 application, but it nevertheless cranked out a healthy 250 horsepower. The unique gunsight taillamps brought an unmistakably aggressive quality.

Series: Mark II

Hardtop coupe

Weight	Price $	Production
4825	9695	2413

Engine

Type	V-8
Displacement (ci.)	368
Bore × stroke	4.00 × 3.66
Horsepower	285
Compression ratio	10.00:1
Fuel feed	Carter 4-bbl

Any list of the most beautiful American automobiles of the 1950s—or ever, for that matter—must place the 1956–57 Continental Mark II very near the top. In preparation from 1953, the car essentially ignored Cadillac and Chrysler's developing Imperial division. Instead, the Mark II was intended to be Ford Motor Company's successor to the 1940–48 Mark I and, perhaps, a challenge even to Rolls-Royce. To that end, the 218.5-inch coupe, riding a 126-inch wheelbase, was the first offering from a new division, Continental, headed by Bill Ford, brother of Henry Ford II.

The final design—with a simple diecast grille, dramatic beltline kick-up at the broad C-pillar, and a smoothly integrated "Continental" spare that was part of the trunklid stamping—resulted from an in- and out-of-house competition involving, from Ford, Gordon Buehrig, John Reinhart, Bill Ford, and Harley Copp; outside teams included A. B. "Buzz" Grisinger/Rees Miller, Walter Buell Ford, Vince Gardner, and George Walker. Each team worked from identical measurements, prepared drawings of the same views (front, rear, side, and three-quarter front/rear), and used the same palette: deep blue with tan interiors. All drawings were scaled to a single size and were judged "blind." The competition was won by the in-house team from Ford.

A unique "cow belly" frame dipped low between the front and rear axles, allowing high seating without a concomitant elevation of the roofline. Practicality and beauty had both been served.

A 368-cid V-8 developed 285 horsepower for 1956, and 300 for '57. Each engine was selected from the Lincoln assembly line and balanced by hand.

Although the interiors were richly finished, they also were simple and functional, in the manner of contemporaneous aircraft and locomotive designs.

The Continental Mark II came to market with a $10,000 price tag, making it the one of the most expensive American automobiles of its day.

Production for 1956 was 2413, and just 576 for 1957—insufficient to justify this magnificent car's continued production.

American auto design after 1955 was certainly not known for consistent and quiet good taste—and yet that's what the '56 Continental Mark II epitomized. Oh, and elegance, too. Stunningly well-shaped and proportioned, this quietly aggressive car was a marvel of careful fit and finish inside and out. Ford executives, designers, and engineers who thought the car might legitimately challenge Rolls-Royce weren't spouting nonsense. The Mark II was frankly brilliant. With a price tag just south of $10,000, the fact that more than 2500 were sold during the first year is remarkable. But that didn't satisfy FoMoCo accountants, who suggested the car be killed after 1957.

Series: Fury		
Hardtop coupe		
Weight	Price $	Production
3650	2866	4485
Engine		
Type	V-8	
Displacement (ci.)	303	
Bore × stroke	3.82 × 3.31	
Horsepower	240	
Compression ratio	9.25:1	
Fuel feed	Carter 4-bbl	

Although not inexpensive at $2866, the 1956 Plymouth Fury was a reasonably priced—and emphatic—response to sister division Chrysler's "super stock" C-300.

A 303-cid polyspherical-head V-8 (not a Hemi) sourced from Chrysler Canada's Dodge Royal was massaged with high-lift cam, solid valve lifters, domed pistons, four-barrel carburetor, free-flow dual exhausts, and 9.25:1 compression—which gave 240 horsepower, or .08 hp per cubic inch. No lightweight at 3650 pounds, the Fury (riding a 115-inch wheelbase) nevertheless could run from zero to 60 in 9.0 seconds and hit 120 mph flat out (a pre-production prototype at Daytona ripped through the flying mile at 124 mph).

The car shared its conventional hardtop coupe body with Savoy and Belvedere but rode an inch lower than its stablemates, on heavy-duty shocks and springs. A front anti-sway bar, 11-inch-diameter Dodge brakes, and wide 7.10 3 15 tires contributed to agile handling.

Fury was readily identified by its standard eggshell-white finish and full-length bodyside sweepspear of gold anodized aluminum. Anodized gold also decorated the grille center and the turbine-spoke wheel covers. This car has wires.

A three-speed manual transmission was standard; a two-speed, pushbutton Powerflite automatic was optional. The dash was standard '56, except for a tachometer that filled the space to the right of the speedometer.

Displacement of the 303 V-8 notched in at the high end of NASCAR's Class 5 (259–305-cid) displacement limit, but when NASCAR ruled that Fury hadn't been in production for the required 90 days and couldn't qualify as "stock," the car was barred from the February 1956 Daytona Speed Weeks. Plymouth responded by campaigning a beefed-up "Factory Experimental" Fury that roared to a top speed of 143.6 mph.

Fury was the first performance Plymouth. It saw production of 4485 and set the table for the hi-po image cultivated by the division in the Sixties.

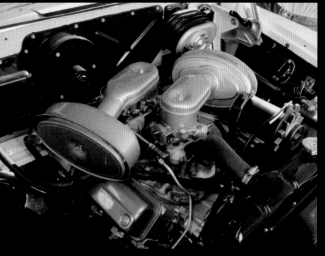

Plymouth introduced the Fury for 1956 and would perpetuate it as a model or separate series through 1989. For '56, Plymouth Division intended the Fury as a performance jewel that would put an end to the make's stodgy image and attract shoppers to Plymouth showrooms. (The car seen here has dealer-installed dual-quad carburetors.) The Fury accomplished those tasks, bringing Plymouth a performance image that the make would capitalize on a decade later. Immediately postwar, Chrysler Corporation chairman K. T. Keller insisted that the company's cars be "tall enough to get into while wearing a hat"—and so they were, to the detriment of style. A fifth-place industry finish for calendar-year 1954 became fourth place with restyled '55s, and another fourth place for '56. And even better days were to come.

Series: Fairlane 500		
Retractable convertible coupe		
Weight	**Price $**	**Production**
3916	2942	20,766
Engine		
Type	V-8	
	V-8	
Displacement (ci.)	272	
	312	
Bore × stroke	3.62 × 3.30	
	3.80 × 3.44	
Horsepower	190	
	300	
Compression ratio	8.60:1	
	9.70:1	
Fuel feed	Holley 2-bbl	
	Holley 4-bbl	

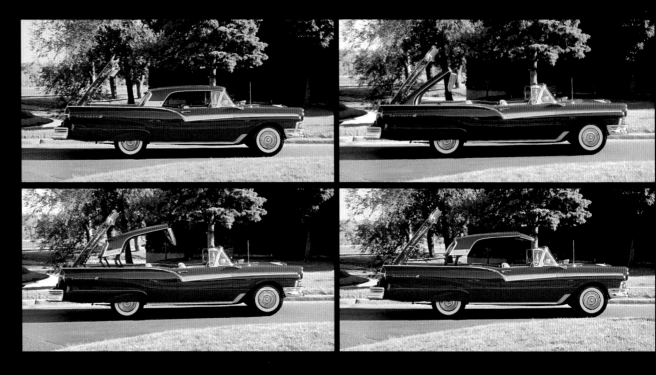

At $2942, the new-for-1957 Fairlane 500 Skyliner retractable-hardtop convertible was far and away the year's most expensive Ford in a year that brought the biggest, most powerful Fords yet. For its debut year, Skyliner managed a pretty fair production run of 20,766 units.

William Clay Ford, head of FoMoCo's Special Projects Division, had been sufficiently impressed by an early hardtop-convertible concept by designer Gilbert Spear that he set aside $2.2 million in development money for creation of a retractable-hardtop '57 Continental Mark II. As things developed, the Mark IIs were standard hardtops only, but Spear's idea was adopted for use—to the tune of another $18 million— by Ford Division.

Because of the power top and the mechanicals needed to operate it, the Skyliner's rear deck stretched three inches longer than that of standard Fairlanes. The space contained 600 feet of wiring, 10 power relays, eight circuit breakers, 10 limit switches, three drive motors, and a safety interlock that inhibited operation if the transmission was in anything but Neutral.

A motor lifted the long decklid via twin side shafts, locking the deck and tripping another motor that elevated the package shelf to deck level. This started yet another motor, which unlocked the top, after which two more motors hoisted the roof and sent it into the enormous cavity below. As the roof was eased downward, a separate servo folded the deck flap.

As you might imagine, luggage space was severely limited, and the panoply of motors and servos could develop gremlins.

Ford Division chief Robert McNamara disliked what he regarded as "gimmick engineering" and tolerated the Skyliner for only three seasons.

Throughout its life, Skyliner was the only Ford with a standard V-8: a 190-horse 272 for 1957, and a 200/205-hp 292 for 1958–59.

Production was 20,766 for 1957, fell to 14,713 for '58, and receded again to 12,915 for '59.

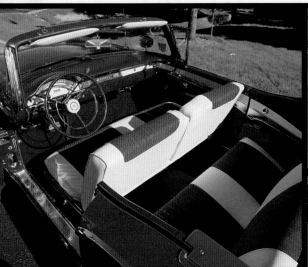

With its short greenhouse and extra-long deck, the '57 Skyliner was as dramatic-looking a car as the marque produced at any time during the decade. The Skyliner was completely unique, too, as it was the world's first mass-produced retractable hardtop. The decklid was hinged in the only possible way, at the back; the top was hinged 10 inches from the front to create a space-saving flap that folded under as it slid back. Even the convertible chassis had to be modified with closer-set side rails to leave room for the top's control linkage. Impressively, little rear legroom was lost. This example has a 300-hp, supercharged version of Ford's 312-cid V-8 that was a rare option for 1957.

Series: Bel Air		
Impala hardtop coupe		
Impala convertible coupe		
Weight	**Price $**	**Production**
3458	2586	125,480 (est.)
3522	2734	55,989 (est.)
Engine		
Type		inline-6 (standard)
		V-8 (standard)
		V-8 (optional)
Displacement (ci.)		235.5
		283.0
		348.0
Bore × stroke		3.56 × 3.94
		3.88 × 3.00
		4.13 × 3.25
Horsepower		145
		185/290
		250/315
Compression ratio		8.25:1
		8.50:1
		9.50:1/11.0:1
Fuel feed		Rochester 1-bbl
		Rochester 2-bbl/4-bbl/FI
		Rochester 4-bbl/three 2-bbl

The 1958 Chevy line was a reflection of America's growing postwar middle class. A worker with a high school diploma, or no diploma at all, could find security in the nation's manufacturing economy. Chevy fed into this affluence with the '58s, which rode a 117.5-inch wheelbase instead of the 115-inchers of 1955–57. The cars now were longer overall (209.1 inches as opposed to the earlier 200), as well as wider, heavier, and lower. Chevy Division knew that increasing numbers of buyers were moving up to Oldsmobile and Buick, and that a perception of luxury—at less cost—was one way to keep those buyers in Chevrolets.

The '58 Chevys were striking, vaguely unusual-looking cars, with a wrapped backlight to go along with a wraparound windshield. The Impala hardtop—part of a new Bel Air subseries— had a lower, shorter greenhouse and a longer deck than other non-wagon models. All sedans and hardtops bore backslanting C-pillars that recalled the '51 Kaiser. All the '58s had sensuous fender tops that flowed into rounded fins canted around and beneath the taillights—three to a side on Impala, a design identifier that would become an Impala hallmark for years to come.

Chrome was generous (Impala "pitchfork" trim ahead of the rear wheels was a lively touch) but far from excessive for the era.

Model-year 1958 also brought Chevrolet's first quad headlights and the division's first big-block V-8, a 348-cid unit that developed 315 horsepower in solid-lifter triple-carb trim. Thus kitted out, this engine zipped from zero to 60 in 7.2 seconds in a *Sports Car Illustrated* road test—quite quick for the day.

Although future "big" Chevys would approximate the size of this one, the '58 was a one-year-only design—a decision made after Chevy designers got an early inkling of what Chrysler was planning for 1957, knowledge that prompted a fresh plan for the '59 Chevy.

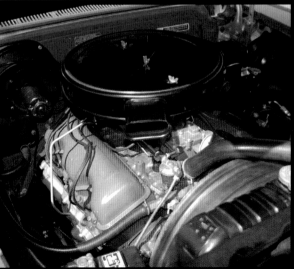

General Motors produced a lot of crazily overwrought cars for 1958—the '58 Buick shuffles to mind—but although the all-new '58 Chevy Impala sported plenty of chrome and eccentric design touches, it had an integrity that eluded some of its GM stablemates. To be sure, it was the result of corporate risk: Work on the '58s began in 1955, another year of great change at Chevy, and at a moment before the sales success of those cars was apparent. Chevy's 1955–57 generation had reached a natural conclusion, and because GM had been caught napping by Chrysler's dramatic "New Look" that debuted for 1957, Chevy knew its '58s had better be similarly long, low, and wide. But where the Chrysler product was all fins and angles, the Chevrolet, though aggressive, was defined by feminized shapes.

Series: 290		
Convertible roadster		
Weight	**Price $**	**Production**
2793	3631	9168
Engine		
Type	V-8	
Displacement (ci.)	283	
Bore × stroke	3.88 × 3.00	
Horsepower	230	
	245/270	
	250/290	
Compression ratio	9.50:1	
Fuel feed	Carter 4-bbl FI	

By 1956, the Corvette was a legitimate sports car, running with a 265-cid V-8 that produced 225 horsepower and capable of leaping from zero to 60 mph in 7.3 seconds.

But sales were small, as witnesses Corvette's 1955–56 total of hardly more than 9800 units. That was weak tea, indeed, even for a niche car, and especially for one that was being pummeled on the sales floor by Ford's Thunderbird.

Ironically (but logically), it was largely because of the dollar and PR potential GM saw in Thunderbird that Corvette was given a reprieve in September 1955, when planning for the 1958 model began.

The self-consciously Space Age 1956 Oldsmobile Golden Rocket show car was to have been the takeoff point for the '58 'Vette. Because Chevy engineers were suddenly needed elsewhere, the Rocket motion was abandoned–and that's for the best because a Rocket-based '58 Corvette would have removed the car from its design roots years before the all-new 1963, and without any of the style continuity of that change.

As things developed, the 1958 Corvette was a natural–if rather flamboyant–follow-on to the 1955–57 series. The 283-cid V-8 that arrived for 1957 now produced 250 horsepower, or 290 with fuel injection.

The car's low, forward-thrust stance carried on. The beautiful and dramatic side coves remained, though now with vertical forward dummy air vents and horizontal windsplits. Single headlamps became quad units circled in wider chrome that now extended back along the fendertops almost to the windscreen.

The toothy grille was toothier still, with wraparound bumperettes that bisected a mysterious, gaping cove beneath each headlight unit.

Sales for 1958 increased by more than 2800 over 1957, and by another 500 units for '59.

Even America's Sports Car was infected by the chromitis that swept through GM when the '58 models were being designed. The ailment led to twin vertical chrome strips on the Corvette's trunk lid, nonfunctional strakes in the bodyside coves, a toothy grille, heavy chrome headlight surrounds, and other dubious embellishments. Much of that was carried forward onto the '59 'Vettes, too, with the result that these cars remain the subjects of lively debate. For '58, Corvette was 10 inches longer than before and more than two inches wider. Bumpers were strengthened, passengers now had a grab bar, and gauges and controls sat directly in front of the driver, instead of spreading out along the dash. It was the best and flashiest Corvette to date. This example runs with fuel injection.

Series: Citation		
Hardtop coupe		
Convertible coupe		
Weight	**Price $**	**Production**
4136	3535	2535
4311	3801	930
Engine		
Type	V-8	
Displacement (ci.)	410	
Bore × stroke	4.20 × 3.70	
Horsepower	345	
Compression ratio	10.50:1	
Fuel feed	4-bbl carburetor	

N othing was fundamentally wrong with the Edsel. Even taking the oddball grille into consideration, the Edsel (named for Clara and Henry Ford's only child) was hardly more overstyled than other American autos of 1958, and it offered the mix of satisfying performance and mediocre braking and handling that was typical of the era. Edsel could be purchased in a variety of series and body styles (too many, probably), with two-tone paint and with varying combinations of V-8 engines and automatic transmissions (with Tele-Touch selector buttons in the steering wheel hub). In all of this, Edsel was very much a car of its time.

Its only failure, and a fatal one, was that it entered a market that Ford had misjudged, mainly on issues of price and consumer desire.

FoMoCo operated five divisions in 1958: Continental, Lincoln, Edsel, Mercury, and Ford. The Edsel-Mercury relationship turned out to be critical to Edsel's fate because the parent company failed to distinguish Edsel from Merc in terms of price and prestige. Mercury was pricier than Ford, and Edsel's Pacer and Ranger wagons, though also more expensive than Fords, were gussied-up Fords. And Edsel's '58 Citation and Corsair models were retrimmed Mercs—so what was the point? Why was there an Edsel at all?

Drop the '58 recession into the mix, and Edsel was doomed.

The short-wheelbase Ranger and Pacer Edsels were expected to be the bread-and-butter Edsels, with the uplevel Corsair and top-dog Citation sitting as the prestige models. The latter two came standard with a 410-cid V-8 producing 345 horsepower and rode a fulsome 124-inch wheelbase.

The three Citation models—hardtop coupe, hardtop sedan, and ragtop coupe—ranged in price from $3535 to $3801. That was the same territory as the DeSoto Fireflite, Chrysler Saratoga, Dodge Coronet D-500, Oldsmobile Super 88, Pontiac Bonneville, and, tellingly, the Mercury Montclair.

Citation was offered only for 1958, accounting for 8577 of the 63,100 Edsels produced for the model year.

Edsel was neither awful nor terrific, and there was nothing about its fate that was preordained. It had the ordinary luck of being a faintly pleasing but ordinary car in a sea of ordinary cars, and the bad luck to arrive during a serious economic recession. Those things, plus buyer confusion as to the reason for its existence, doomed it. As one historian wrote, "Its aim was right but the target moved." But when Edsel was conceived in 1954, the medium-price market was booming, so a line to complement Mercury—and give Ford Motor Co. another division with which to challenge GM—seemed to make perfect sense. Pontiac, Buick, and Dodge were producing cars in record numbers, helping to boost the medium-price market to 25 percent of the total. When Edsel was introduced, that share had shriveled to 18 percent. Plus, there was that horse collar grille!

Series: Thunderbird		
Hardtop coupe		
Convertible coupe		
Weight	**Price $**	**Production**
3876	3631	35,758
3944	3929	2134
Engine		
Type	V-8	
Displacement (ci.)	352	
Bore × stroke	4.00 × 3.59	
Horsepower	300	
Compression ratio	9.10:1	
Fuel feed	Holley 4-bbl	

R ather unexpectedly, Ford Division general manager Robert McNamara expressed support in 1955 for the Thunderbird. But he wasn't enamored of the T-bird's two-seat configuration and niche status. What he valued was the growing equity of the Thunderbird name, which he figured could be leveraged into a four-place 'Bird.

That's precisely what happened for 1958, and although sports car purists howled (some are howling still), the 1958–60 Thunderbird was a beautiful, swift, and sportive car with smartly crisp lines that earned it the affectionate nickname "Squarebird." It was also a significant force in the new "personal-luxury" segment that would blossom later with Mustang, Buick's '63 Riviera, and others.

In a reversal of normal practice, Ford Division's design department, headed by Bill Boyer, laid down the basics of the new Thunderbird—not the staff in engineering. Ground clearance of just 5.8 inches mandated a high transmission tunnel that Boyer's people turned into the car's primary longitudinal structural unit. Further, as far as Squarebird occupants were concerned, the hump was a smart-looking console fitted with climate controls, power-window switches, and a radio speaker.

Additional rigidity came from a massive cowl, a reinforced rear deck and rear quarter panels, and chassis rails riding six inches deep to create a recessed cabin floor. Unibody construction and an all-coil Ford-Aire suspension also contributed to this very competent package.

The sole engine was a potent 352-cid V-8 rated at 300 horsepower, mated to a column-mounted three-speed manual, a manual with optional overdrive, or three-speed dual-range Cruise-O-Matic. Famed *Mechanix Illustrated* tester "Uncle" Tom McCahill ran a '58 'Bird from zero to 60 in 9.9 seconds—good for the day, particularly for a car that weighed the better part of two tons.

The hardtop coupe could be had for $3631 in 1958; the convertible coupe for $3929. By 1960, prices ranged from $3755 to $4222, with sales healthier than ever.

Offered as a convertible and a hardtop coupe (the latter a first for Thunderbird), the four-place '58 was a smashing success that found nearly 38,000 buyers—up from about 21,300 for the '57, which was the last of the two-seat T-birds. Clearly, the car's combination of sportiness and luxury encouraged people to buy. Despite the '58's fairly revolutionary nature, Ford Division set aside only $5 million for design and body/chassis engineering, plus another $2 million for body changes through 1960. Cost overruns on convertible development ate up the second sum, so the 1959 Thunderbird was virtually unchanged from the '58. Main differences: optional availability of the 350-hp Lincoln 430 V-8 and, late in the season, a standard, fully automatic top for the ragtop. Nineteen sixty brought a busier grille and an extra-cost sliding steel sunroof for the hardtop.

Series: 62		
Eldorado Seville hardtop coupe		
Biarritz convertible coupe		
Hardtop coupe		
Convertible coupe		
Weight	**Price $**	**Production**
4855	7401	975
5058	7401	1320
4690	4892	21,947
4855	5455	11,130
Engine		
Type	V-8	
Displacement (ci.)	390	
Bore × stroke	4.00 × 3.88	
Horsepower	325/345	
Compression ratio	10.50:1	
Fuel feed	three Rochester 2-bbl	
	Rochester 4-bbl	

The '59 Cadillac is a flamboyant car that makes poor use of interior space and hogs enormous sections of highway. But it's also a perfect expression of Eisenhower-era American optimism. The '59 Cadillac was born in a country where, for an illusory moment, all things seemed possible.

The great hallmark of this car is, of course, its towering tail fins and those outthrust, sci-fi taillights. These Chrysler-influenced protuberances—plus the bejeweled front and rear grilles, jet-like "exhaust ports" that housed the backup lights, and the car's sheer presence—comprise what's best recalled about the '59.

The almost subliminal straight-through line that describes the car from front to back happened because GM economics demanded that the expensively redesigned front doors of the new 1959 Buick become interchangeable elements of C-body design. The Buick doors tapered rearward, encouraging Cadillac design chief Ed Glowacke, studio designer Dave Holls, and others to taper the entire Cadillac bodyside. This—more than the fins, really—is what gives these cars the illusion of movement when they're standing still.

Style aside, the '59 Caddy had some good engineering. A tubular-center X-frame brought solidity and allowed the car to ride low on its 130-inch wheelbase (149.8 on the Fleetwood Seventy-Five). Standard Hydra-Matic was mated to a muscular 390-cid ohv V-8 that developed 325 horsepower on most models, and a robust 345 on the Eldorado series comprising a Seville hardtop coupe, Biarritz convertible, and a showcar-inspired Brougham hardtop sedan. Eleven total models (including two convertibles) spanned a weight range from 4690 pounds to a staggering 5570. That's serious heft, and yet lighter examples could run from zero to 60 in 11.5 seconds. Power steering and power brakes were standard.

On the debit side, fit and finish was less than sterling, and the cars' front ends were prone to vibration and chatter. Some trim pieces looked a little low-rent, and the '59 was susceptible to rust.

An imperfect American icon. Imagine.

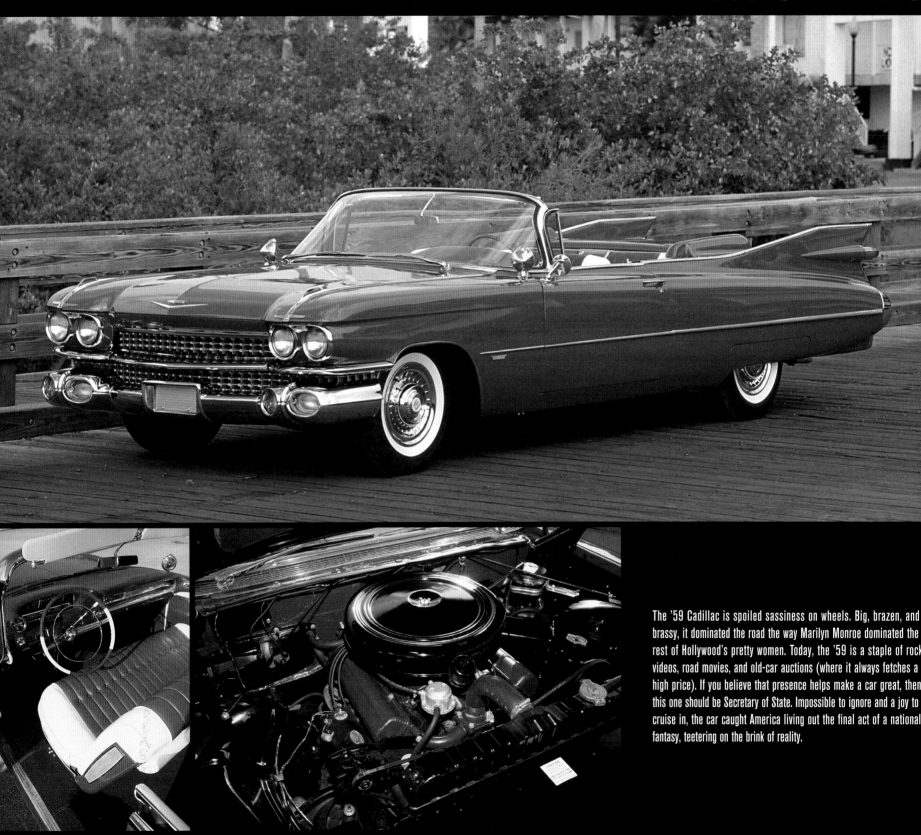

The '59 Cadillac is spoiled sassiness on wheels. Big, brazen, and brassy, it dominated the road the way Marilyn Monroe dominated the rest of Hollywood's pretty women. Today, the '59 is a staple of rock videos, road movies, and old-car auctions (where it always fetches a high price). If you believe that presence helps make a car great, then this one should be Secretary of State. Impossible to ignore and a joy to cruise in, the car caught America living out the final act of a national fantasy, teetering on the brink of reality.

Series: Continental		
Hardtop sedan		
Convertible sedan		
Weight	**Price $**	**Production**
4927	6067	22,303
5215	6713	2857
Engine		
Type	V-8	
Displacement (ci.)	430	
Bore × stroke	4.30 × 3.70	
Horsepower	300/320	
Compression ratio	10.00:1	
Fuel feed	Carter 2-bbl (300 hp)	
	Carter 4-bbl (320 hp)	

I n a provocative 2004 article for the *Daily Telegraph* of London, British author and design critic Stephen Bayley wrote, "…I am more than ever convinced that the great figures [of modern sculpture] include Eugene Bordinat, Don DeLaRossa, Elwood P. Engel, Gale L. Halderman, John Najjar, Robert M. Thomas and George Walker."

Bayley was concerned about the schizophrenic state of serious sculpture, but in the work of the men he mentioned, Bayley saw clarity of intent and purity of design.

None of the seven men were sculptors in the commonly accepted sense, but they nevertheless created an enduring work of art: the 1961 Lincoln Continental.

With smooth, completely uncluttered bodysides; bright metal fender strips that ran uninterrupted from front to rear; and a full-width yet subtle grille culminating in quad headlights, the Continental bespoke sophisticated elegance.

Intriguingly, the Continental shared tooling for its entire front structure with the freshly redesigned '61 "rocket" Thunderbird, without any noticeable resemblance. Riding a 123-inch wheelbase (113 for the 'Bird), the Continental was a four-door sedan or convertible that stretched 212.4 inches overall. Rear doors were back-hinged and opened "suicide" style, on both body styles, for easy egress, and the high fendertops remained in the driver's view, for added confidence during tight maneuvering.

Harold MacDonald, Ford Division's chief engineer, brought marked improvements to unit-body and chassis rigidity, sound insulation, and shock damping. All mechanical components were machined to exacting tolerances.

Every 430-cid, 300/320 horsepower V-8 was run for three hours at 3500 rpm on a dynamometer, and then torn down, inspected, and reassembled. A 12-mile road test followed.

The redesigned Continental saw production of 25,160 units for 1961, about double the previous year's total. The figures continued to rise, more modestly, for carry-on years 1962 and '63, and put Lincoln in front of Chrysler's Imperial for good.

Spec requirements demanded that the engine of the '61 Lincoln Continental be situated very close to the firewall, which would have created an enormous transmission hump that intruded into the passenger compartment. That would have reduced the Continental's passenger capacity from six to four, and that just wasn't acceptable. Because the driveline of the earlier Continental Mark II had a tendency to vibrate, Harold MacDonald, the division's chief engineer, contracted with Dana Corporation to come up with an inexpensive constant-velocity, double-cardin universal joint. Dana obliged, and although the technology was never used on the Mark II, it was revived for the '61 Continental, allowing the transmission and propeller shaft to be angled downward. This way, the 123-inch- wheelbase Conti still seated six.

Series: Galaxie 500		
XL Victoria hardtop coupe		
XL Sunliner convertible coupe		
Weight	**Price $**	**Production**
3672	2268	28,412
3831	3518	13,183
Engine		
Type	V-8	
	V-8	
	V-8	
	V-8	
Displacement (ci.)	292	
	352	
	390	
	406	
Bore × stroke	3.75 × 3.30	
	4.00 × 3.50	
	4.05 × 3.78	
	4.13 × 3.78	
Horsepower	170	
	220	
	300	
	385/405	
Compression ratio	8.80:1	
	8.90:1	
	9.60:1	
	11.30:1	
Fuel feed	Holley 2-bbl	
	Holley 2-bbl	
	Holley 4-bbl	
	three Holley 2-bbl or	
	Holley 4-bbl	

nitially, the standard engine/transmission setup on the facelifted '62 Ford Galaxie XL (ostensibly for "Xtra Lively," a Galaxie 500 subseries comprising the Victoria hardtop coupe and Sunliner convertible) was a 170-horse, 292-cid V-8 mated to Cruise-O-Matic. But when Ford general manager Lee Iacocca realized that performance was going to count for as much in the marketplace as looks, the Galaxie picked up three optional eights: a 352 rated at 220 hp, a 390 producing 300 hp, and a NASCAR-intentioned 406-cid unit with a thumping 385 or 405 horsepower, with a four-barrel carb or three two-barrels, respectively.

A *Motor Trend* test Galaxie with the 406 ripped from zero to 60 mph in 7.1 seconds, and the magazine estimated top speed at a heady 140.

A standard Galaxie cost $2674 for 1962, with the XL upping the tab to $3108—not inexpensive for the day.

A reskin for "Super Torque" 1963 brought a leaner, lower look and a concave grille with newly tightened mesh. The base engine shrank to a 260-cid, 164-hp V-8 but was shortly replaced by a 289 rated at 195 hp. Top engine now was a 406 re-bored to 427-cubic-inch displacement, for 410/425 hp. But these big motors were expensive at about $400 and relatively few were ordered.

A two-door '63 Sports hardtop that arrived at mid-year flaunted a thin-pillar, slantback roof and was intended by Ford corporate to excite interest among stock-car racers.

The dramatically reskinned '64 XL, with heavily sculptured lower-body sheet metal and a busy grille, cornered well and was pleasing when fitted with the more muscular power packages. But these were heavy, full-size cars that were due for a squared-up redesign for 1965. A bit later in the decade, these and other full-size runners would be replaced on the wish lists of buffs by a variety of muscular midsizes.

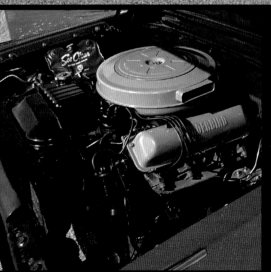

There's something exciting about a heavy, full-size car that has the wherewithal to rip past just about any, ostensibly sportier, challenger. Ford's Galaxie XL sold good looks and luxury, but it also epitomized Ford's publicly stated credo: "Racing improves the breed." In other words, create stock cars that can be successfully campaigned and additional powertrain and other tech advances will follow. And racing success usually helped sales, too. Ford division's new general manager, a gent named Lee Iacocca, was a great believer in the race mantra and launched an all-out assault on motorsports titles and records. Ford called this "Total Performance," which was the company's first shot in the Baby Boomer wars. By 1962, the oldest Boomers were 16—old enough to drive and old enough to talk Mom and Dad into buying a full-size flyer.

Series: Riviera

Riviera hardtop coupe

Weight	Price $	Production
3988	4333	40,000

Engine

Type	V-8
Displacement (ci.)	401
	425
Bore × stroke	4.19 × 3.64
	4.31 × 3.64
Horsepower	325
	340
Compression ratio	10.25:1
Fuel feed	4-bbl carburetor

G eneral Motors design chief Bill Mitchell was nearly as fond of aircraft cues as his predecessor, Harley Earl, but the shared little of Earl's love for great slathers of chrome, exaggerated body contours, and nonfunctional styling doodads. Mitchell wanted to guide GM to a new aesthetic, and he did—with a Buick that was originally conceived as a revival of LaSalle, Cadillac's lower-priced companion make of 1927–40.

The sales success of Ford's 1958 Thunderbird—a complete "Squarebird" re-do that added two more seats and steered the 'Bird from sports car to personal-luxury ride—didn't go unnoticed by General Motors. Ford had uncovered a new market segment and tapped into it with verve.

GM concepts of the late Fifties that might inspire a counter to the T-Bird left Mitchell unimpressed. Chief Buick designer Ned Nickles felt the same way; like Mitchell, he had no patience for self-conscious Buck Rogers futurism. With Mitchell's encouragement, Nickles came up with a concept called XP-715. Because Buick sales had slipped from third to ninth in overall sales between 1955 and 1960, the new concept went to that division. Finally going on sale as the '63 Riviera late in 1962, the car rode a discrete 117-inch wheelbase and was about 14 inches shorter and 200–300 pounds lighter than its typical Buick stablemate. GM's X-member chassis with all-coil suspension rightly suggested that under the skin, Riviera was conventional. Drum brakes had power assist, and power steering was standard.

The Riv comported itself fairly well in hard cornering and was a pleasant surprise in the 0-to-60 sprint: about 9.0 seconds. By 1964, the Riv's top 425-cid V-8 produced 360 horsepower and shaved nearly a second from the run-up to 60 mph.

The car's startling appeal really lay in its design: curvaceous without being blowsy, with relatively unadorned bodysides and an elegant, forward-thrust nose with a contoured blade bumper. Hidden headlamps arrived for 1965. Smart and luxurious, the first-generation Riviera still looks stunning today.

Cadillac's junior make, LaSalle (1927–40), helped keep Caddy alive during the Depression, so GM's fondness for the name was understandable. "LaSalle" was a 1955 Motorama show car, and for a while it was going to be the name of the new Buick that became the '63 Riviera (an existing Buick name in use since 1949). The 1962 Riviera was a 4448-pound six-window hardtop sedan on a 126-inch wheelbase. For 1963, the redesigned Riv kept the hardtop body style but was made considerably more svelte. And it was, of course, a two-door. The design, which was supervised by Bill Mitchell, appeared for the same model year as another Mitchell triumph, the '63 Corvette Sting Ray.

Series: Sting Ray		
Sting Ray coupe		
Weight	**Price $**	**Production**
2859	4252	10,594

Engine	
Type	V-8
Displacement (ci.)	327
Bore × stroke	4.00 × 3.25
Horsepower	250
	300/340
	360
Compression ratio	10.50:1
Fuel feed	Carter 4-bbl FI

E verybody loves a convertible, but the fact is that no convertible Corvette has ever been as gorgeous as Bill Mitchell and Larry Shinoda's '63 "split-window" Sting Ray (two words, thank you) coupe. The car inaugurated Corvette's second generation and was a dramatic break from styling that, in fundamental ways, had changed but little since 1953. Hidden headlamps, sharply creased front fenders, a sleek and aggressive vertical prow on the hood, rear fenders that were at once subtle and pugnacious, split blade bumpers—and that dramatically raked two-piece backlight that tapered to a point, just above the rear bumper. The window's center divider did nothing to improve visibility, but the boat tail deck brought a Space Age spin to a feature that recalled Auburns, Packards, and other design trendsetters of the Classic Era.

The new car was trimmer too, riding a 98-inch wheelbase rather than the previous 102-inch setup. The 327 V-8 carried over from 1962, still rated at 250/300/340 horsepower with carburetors, and 360 hp with fuel injection.

Displacement and output subsequently increased, so that by 1967—the final year of this generation—top hp, from a 427-cid V-8, was a thumping 435. Through the five years of the Sting Ray's run, top speed muscled-up from 118 mph to 152.

Four-wheel disc brakes became available for 1965, and when the big block arrived, side pipes for drivers with a hey-look-at-me inclination showed up, too.

Nineteen sixty-two production of 14,531 had been far and away the best ever for Corvette, but the '63 mark of 21,515 blew the previous year's total out of the water. Second-generation Sting Ray production peaked in 1966, at 27,720.

In an ironic turn of events, it wasn't uncommon for owners of '63s to remove the two-piece backlight and replace it with the sort of single-pane affair that arrived for 1964. The owners' rearward vision got better, but the future value of their cars took a tumble.

The '63 Sting Ray isn't the most gorgeous car ever built, but it's definitely in the running. Because it is a natural-enough follow-on to the last of the first-generation 'Vettes, it's appreciated for its seemingly effortless blend of audaciousness and evolutionary design logic. But it's also like a glorious, unfamiliar machine airlifted to us from another planet. And Sting Ray was as new to Corvette as it was to admirers, as it was the first-ever Corvette coupe. Some owners complained about rearward visibility, but that one-year-only split window was product "branding" at its purest and most sincere. A 1963 Chevy ad said, "The car you drive reflects who you are to the world. Aside from its dramatic looks and vivid performance, the new Corvette Sting Ray imparts an aura of individuality to its owners."

Series: Avanti		
Sport coupe		
Weight	Price $	Production
3140	4445	3834
Engine		
Type	V-8	
	V-8	
Displacement (ci.)	289	
	289 supercharged	
Bore × stroke	3.56 × 3.63	
	3.56 × 3.63	
Horsepower	240	
	290	
Compression ratio	10.25:1	
	9.00:1	
Fuel feed	Carter 4-bbl	
	Carter 4-bbl	

S tudebaker entered its final downward spiral after 1960, but before closing its old South Bend, Indiana, plant to consolidate production in Hamilton, Ontario, late in 1963, it produced the Avanti, a well-wrought specialty car that, unfortunately, was not the car Studebaker needed at that moment.

Before Avanti entered development, two factions dominated Studebaker. One, led by company president Harold Churchill, wanted to lay the foundation for sustainable, broad-appeal growth by building on the success of the compact Lark. Others within the company, though, wanted to expand the product line with, among other things, a niche car that would become a symbol of company vision. The latter faction forced Churchill's ouster in 1961 and his replacement by Sherwood Egbert.

In Italian, "avanti" means "forward," which is a fair summation of the fiberglass-bodied, four-place coupe created by John Ebstein, Robert Andrews, and Tom Kellogg for famed designer Raymond Loewy. It was a long-hood/short-deck car with a nose strikingly devoid of a grille (air intakes were partially hidden beneath the bumper); a massive, curved rear window; and elevated haunches that suggested a cat about to spring.

Because time and money were precious, the Avanti body rode a Lark convertible chassis strengthened with roll bars front and rear, rear radius rods, and Bendix front-disc power brakes, which had become newly optional for Stude's Lark and Hawk.

The company's existing 289-cid V-8 was bumped from 225 horsepower to 240, to become the standard Avanti engine. An optional, supercharged variant roused 290 horses. Top speed was 115–120 mph, and zero to 60 could be accomplished in 7.0–8.0 seconds—very fast for the day.

Buyers lined up for Avanti, but trouble with the fiberglass slowed manufacture, and many orders were lost. In the end, 3824 Avantis were produced for 1963.

Changes for 1964 (restyled parking lights and, on most cars, square-bezel headlight surrounds) were cosmetic, and only 809 second-season Avantis were produced.

Stude made no Avantis after December 1963, but the name and body style continued via a succession of independent makers.

Out-of-house designer Raymond Loewy wowed Studebaker executives with a small-scale model of what would become the Avanti; the design was accepted for production, with hardly a change. Loewy promised that the coupe would be the car from which the larger Studebaker line would evolve and profit. But production delays and the generally failing state of Stude's affairs helped keep that from happening. The 290-hp supercharged engine was developed by Andy Granatelli and Paxton Automotive. They also developed a bored-out 304.5-cid version in three higher stages of tune: The experimental top dog was called R5. It had two Paxton superchargers, one for each cylinder bank, plus a magneto ignition and Bendix fuel injection. Output was a boggling 575 horsepower.

Series: 426 Hemi		
Coupe		
Weight	Price $	Production
3210	4600	N/A
Engine		
Type	V-8	
Displacement (ci.)	426	
Bore × stroke	4.25 × 3.75	
Horsepower	425	
Compression ratio	12.50:1	
Fuel feed	two Carter 4-bbl	

At the center of Chrysler's contribution to American high performance is a storied engine of remarkable achievement: the Hemi. The company's original run of Hemi V-8s ended in 1958, with a 390-bhp 392-cid edition. The design was sound—large, hemispherical combustion chambers are highly efficient—but Hemis were complex, heavy, and expensive.

By the early 1960s, stakes were high enough for Chrysler to try again. To win on NASCAR's new superspeedways, and to dominate at the cutting-edge of drag racing, Mopar engineers developed a Hemi based on the 413/426 wedge-head engines. It still was costly and complicated, but the new mill weighed just 67 pounds more than the wedges. Maximum advertised horsepower for the 426-cid Hemi was 425. Rumor had dyno needles breaking at 600 bhp.

These engines were reserved for racing, and their impact was immediate. Debuting at the Daytona 500 in February 1964, they promptly swept the first three places in NASCAR's premier event. Stock-car racing Hemis had a single Holley four-barrel atop a dual-plane high-rise intake manifold and were used with a four-speed manual gearbox. Drag-racing versions had a ram-tuned aluminum induction system with Carter AFB dual quads. Available only in special-order intermediate-size Dodge and Plymouth models, they ran the four-speed or the TorqueFlite automatic, which was in its last year with pushbuttons.

Available from the factory were a series of sub-12-second supercars that used aluminum for the hood, front fenders, doors, and some body panels. A lightened front bumper and magnesium front wheels were standard. The cars had no radio, no heater, no back seat or carpet, no sound-deadening material. Featherweight Dodge van bucket seats were used, the side windows were plastic, and the battery rode in the trunk.

Street versions of the Hemi engine wouldn't be available for a couple of years. But King Kong had arrived.

Arriving in 1964, the 426 Hemi immediately propelled Dodge and Plymouth into NASCAR's winner's circle and into drag-racing dominance. The most-popular Hemi Dodge was the midsize 330/440/Polara. This is a 330 with the Maximum Performance Package. It's a factory-built, Super Stock-class quarter-miler with aluminum body panels and lightweight interior components. The race-Hemi powertrain uses a TorqueFlite with dash-mounted pushbuttons. It wouldn't have been pleasant, but this car was street-legal.

Series: Fairlane

2-door sedan

Weight	Price $	Production
3225 (M)	3780	100
3980 (A)		

Engine

Type	V-8
Displacement (ci.)	427
Bore × stroke	4.23 × 3.78
Horsepower	425
Compression ratio	12.70:1
Fuel feed	two Holley 4-bbl

Domed hoods notwithstanding, Ford Thunderbolts were unassuming-appearing cars that started life as Fairlanes but were transformed into brutes by Dearborn Steel Tubing Company, near Ford headquarters.

Ford wanted to establish a presence on the strip, but its Galaxie XL, although swift on the oval, was too heavy for competitive acceleration on the straight. The Fairlane was smaller and 700 pounds lighter. If it was given a potent engine and stripped of unnecessary weight, it could be a potent drag racer.

So that Ford's High Riser 427 could be accommodated, engineers reworked Fairlane's front suspension and refabricated some of that system's components. The unique hood was made of fiberglass; likewise the doors and front fenders. Early Thunderbolts had fiberglass front bumpers that were switched to aluminum after a National Hot Rod Association ruling. The windshield remained stock, but the backlight and side windows were Plexiglas.

Inside and out, other nonessential items were tossed for weight. Armrests, sun visors, mirrors, jack, lug wrench, radio, heater, carpeting, hubcaps: gone.

The 427 ran with 12.70:1 compression, and although the motor was rated at 425 horsepower, true output may have been as much as 100 horses higher. T-bolt came standard with a Borg-Warner four-speed stick, though many buyers ponied up another hundred bucks for a three-speed automatic adapted from the Lincoln transmission.

On the strip, Thunderbolt blasted through the quarter in the mid-11s, at a blood-stirring 120 to 126 mph. Driver Gas Ronda won the '64 Winternationals with a T-bolt run of 11.6 seconds at 124.38 mph.

A Thunderbolt cost $3780, quite a premium considering that a standard Fairlane started at $2194.

Thunderbolt production totaled 100. The car was sold without warranty, and every buyer had to sign a waiver absolving Ford of responsibility for repairs or personal injury.

According to *Merriam-Webster*, a secondary definition of "beast" is "something formidably difficult to control or deal with." Well, that's fair enough if the topic is the '64 Thunderbolt. The car was street legal, but that business of having to sign a waiver absolving Ford of all blame if you accidentally drove the thing into the side of a building suggested that the T-bolt wasn't exactly docile. But on the strip, you'd bring home trophies. The car's inner headlights were screened so that the big 427 could swallow all the air it needed. The four-speed ran with 4.44:1 gearing, the three-speed automatic with 4.58:1. Heavy-duty rear suspension upgrades and massive traction bars helped get at least 500 horsepower down to the road.

Series: Tempest GTO		
GTO sport coupe		
GTO hardtop coupe		
GTO convertible coupe		

Weight	Price $	Production
3000	3200	7384
3020	3250	18,422
3150	3500	6644

Engine	
Type	V-8
Displacement (ci.)	389
Bore × stroke	4.06 × 3.75
Horsepower	325/348
Compression ratio	10.75:1
Fuel feed	4-bbl carburetor

F or 1964, Pontiac's already innovative Tempest was given GM's new A-body platform that took the car into the mid-size class with a wheelbase stretch of three inches, to 115. Tempest shared the new platform with the Chevy Chevelle, Olds F-85/Cutlass, and Buick Special/Skylark. Although Pontiac dumped Tempest's novel "rope drive" in favor of standard-technology transmissions, the Tempest remained very interesting because it could be had as the GTO (for *Gran Turismo Omologato*), a car so hot that GM policy prohibited it from being offered as a separate model—hence, the first Goat was packaged as an option (about $300) for the '64 Tempest LeMans coupe, convertible, and two-door hardtop.

A lot of this was the brain-child of Jim Wangers, Pontiac's chief marketing manager, who saw a niche for a midsize car with plenty of muscle—and who *insisted* that it be built.

Pontiac general manager "Pete" Estes made sure that the GTO option could in turn be optioned to the stratosphere, with such goodies as heavy-duty three- or four-speed manuals (available with floorshift and Hurst linkage), two-speed Hydra-Matic, limited-slip differential, metallic brake linings, heavy-duty radiator, and side-exit exhaust splitters, plus appearance features and creature comforts such as a vinyl top, center console, power steering/brakes/windows, radio, AC, and whitewall or red-stripe tires.

Pontiac's highly regarded 389-cid V-8—uprated with cylinder heads and other components from GM's 421 "H.O." motor—produced 325/348 horsepower for 1964 and 335/360 for '65. In top trim, a GTO could run from zero to 60 mph in 6.5 seconds and handle the quarter in under 15 seconds at nearly 100 mph.

Pontiac had anticipated selling about 5000 GTO packages for 1964 and was pleasantly shocked when production topped 32,000. For the '65 model year (which brought a freshened grille and stacked quad headlights), production shot past 75,000 units.

Looking more like the Tempest that was under the skin than like the "Goat" it would shortly become, the '64 GTO had a simplicity that was the template for future muscle car development: honkin' big motor and speed features in an otherwise unassuming midsize coupe. Flashy, visible displays of horsepower were still reserved for hot rods, so there was great appeal in the GTO's unassuming garb. Who doesn't like to pilot a stoplight fooler? The real genius of the GTO—and of all subsequent midsize muscle cars—was that it appealed not just to young buyers but served, sans muscle add-ons, as workaday transportation that amortized the performance experiment. With regard to muscle cars, Pontiac was the first automaker to have its cake and eat it too.

Series: Mustang		
Hardtop coupe		
Convertible coupe		
Fastback coupe		

Weight	Price $	Production
2583	2372	501,965
2789	2614	101,945
2633	2589	77,079

Engine	
Type	inline-6
	V-8
	V-8
Displacement (ci.)	200
	289
	289
Bore × stroke	3.68 × 3.13
	4.00 × 2.87
	4.00 × 2.87
Horsepower	120
	225
	271
Compression ratio	9.20:1
	10.00:1
	10.50:1
Fuel feed	Ford Autolite 2-bbl
	Ford Autolite 4-bb
	Ford Autolite 4-bb

Mustang is the car that changed everything, proving the existence of a youth market ready to be turned on by a sporty personal car (Falcon underpinnings notwithstanding) that could be optioned from six-cylinder mild to V-8 wild. It's one of the greatest of all automotive success stories.

The archetypal '65 Mustang is the hardtop coupe, a car that most clearly shows off the aggressive yet pretty long-hood/short-deck proportions by Joe Oros, L. David Ash, and Gale Halderman. The car remains beloved as well as respected, and thousands of examples are proudly driven today. And although clearly a "youth" car, the hardtop's purity of design also lent itself to appeals to chic sophistication.

The '65 Mustang fastback became available on October 1, 1964, fewer than five months after the coupe and convertible (the last, the priciest Mustang, at $2614) appeared in dealerships. Initial fastback badging said "MUSTANG 2+2," and although two people could be squeezed into the back seat beneath the sharply sloped roof, bags of groceries might feel more at home. The side-rear "window" vents were functional air extractors.

Base fastbacks were equipped with a 200-cid, 120-hp inline six, which was sufficient to move the 2589-pound 2+2 around town with OK briskness. Drop in the small-block 289 V-8, though, and you had a different animal altogether. During this first model year, more than 77,000 fastbacks found homes.

The GT (for *Gran Turismo*) was the performance Mustang and was intended to suggest drivers' adventurous, even aggressive, spirits. Most GT packages had the 225-hp 289 with four-barrel carburetor and a three-speed, fully synchronized stick shift. The GT's front disc brakes were particularly useful if the buyer opted for the 271-horse version of the 289, with 4-speed stick (the latter an oxymoronic "mandatory option"). The stronger 289 had optional "short" rear axle ratios (3.89:1 and 4.11:1), which made the cars enormously appealing to street and strip drag racers.

The original Mustang, a 1962 concept called Mustang I, rode a tiny 90-inch wheelbase and ran with an 89-horse V-4. The concept was a logical evolution of Ford Division general manager Lee Iacocca's interest in the nascent youth market. Of the approximately 677,000 regular-production Mustangs built for model-year 1965, more than 100,000 were convertibles. At $2614 base, they were the most expensive first-year Mustangs, offering engines ranging from 120 to 271 horsepower. The Mustang ragtop was an especially keen illustration of Mustang's canny appeal to youth, particularly when running with the small-block 289 mated to a three- or four-speed manual shift. This was youth, this was power, this was the essence of Mustang.

Series: 252 Catalina		
Sport coupe hardtop		
Convertible coupe		
Weight	**Price $**	**Production**
3992	3287	11,521
4039	4039	(total htp/conv)
Engine		
Type	V-8	
Displacement (ci.)	421	
Bore × stroke	4.09 × 4.00	
Horsepower	338/356/376	
Compression ratio	10.75:1	
Fuel feed	three Rochester 2-bbl	
	Rochester 4-bbl	

The story of the 1965–67 Catalina 2+2 really begins in 1964, when a $291 2+2 option became available for Catalina hardtops and convertibles. The package brought a 389 V-8 rated at 267/283 horsepower, bucket seats, center console with a vacuum gauge, unique exterior badges, and a special interior covered in a not-bad imitation-leather vinyl called Morrokide. About 8000 Catalina hardtops and convertibles were produced with the 2+2 package for '64—enough for Pontiac to continue the option. The '65 model year brought extraordinarily shapely redesigns to the full-size Pontiacs and an even livelier 2+2 package for Catalina. The 389 was replaced with the 338/356/376-horsepower 421. Other features of the basic 2+2 package included a three-speed Hurst floor shift, heavy duty shocks and springs, 3.42:1 performance rear axle, chrome engine parts, full wheel discs, fender pinstripes, and unique fender louvers and identifying badges on hood and deck.

The package was a little more pricey now: $419 with Catalina coupes and $397 with convertibles. Buyers who opted for a complete gauge package, a four-speed automatic transmission, and power brakes (front discs optional), windows, and antenna would spend about $4000 for the hardtop.

The 2+2 was a majestic-looking car that was subdued in city driving and a bit of a beast out in the open, where a hardtop example could sprint from zero to 60 in 7.4 seconds and reach 95 mph in the standing-start quarter mile.

The 2+2 earned individual-model status for 1966, and then reverted to a Catalina package for '67, when the base motor was a 428 rated at 360/376 hp.

About 19,600 2+2s were sold during 1965–67. Although the '65s are the most plentiful, they also are the most desired today.

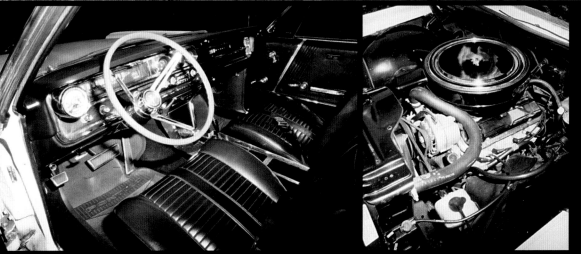

The Catalina 2+2 came at a time when gas was still inexpensive, when it was okay to make inefficient use of space in a sedan-sized coupe, and when "personal luxury" mated to performance was still developing as a marketing concept. The '65 Catalina had presence to begin with and was a gem of fulsome overstatement when running with the potent 2+2 performance package. At 3700–3800 pounds, the 2+2 hardtop and convertible were fleet (if not nimble, despite beefy suspensions). The hood bulge, curved side glass, side vents, and "Venturi" contours on the lower bodysides were new for '65.

Series: Toronado		
Hardtop coupe		
DeLuxe hardtop coupe		
Weight	**Price $**	**Production**
4311	4617	6333
4366	4812	34,630
Engine		
Type	V-8	
Displacement (ci.)	425	
Bore × stroke	4.13 × 3.98	
Horsepower	385	
Compression ratio	10.50:1	
Fuel feed	Rochester 4GC 4-bbl	

Although the original name chosen for the 1936 Cord was Cord "New Front Drive," the factory code, "810," was ultimately adopted. The coffin-nose Cord combined beauty and performance with a novel front-drive layout. Hidden headlights, emphatic fenders and wheelwells, backswept deck, and a bold grille with horizontal louvers marked the Cord as something special.

Flash forward 30 years to GM's Oldsmobile division, and its New Front Drive beauty, the Toronado: hidden headlights; upthrust front fenders; a wide, narrow grille described by thin horizontal bars; bold, flared wheel wells and a down-sloped deck. No, this wasn't an imitation Cord—it neither wanted nor needed to be—but Toronado was nearly as unique as that earlier triumph.

An impressive 54/46 front-rear weight distribution was accomplished via a weight-saving two-piece transmission setup by which the torque converter was mounted behind the engine, with the gearbox located remotely under the left cylinder bank. The components were connected by a very strong, flexible chain drive and sprocket. The whole design allowed a compact engine and drivetrain that cost less to manufacture than traditional transmissions.

Virtually unchanged between 1966 and '67, the Toronado ran with a hardy 425-cid V-8 producing 385 horsepower. The 4300-pound car was no slouch off the line (8.5 seconds, zero to 60) but real pleasure was on the open road, where the Toronado cruised happily at 100 mph.

For a front-driver, understeer was very well controlled, but owners had to become accustomed to the inevitable wear on the front tires. The C-pillars looked elegant, but their width hampered over-the-shoulder visibility, and because the heavy, very long doors were a chore to open and close, a built-in assist was added for '67.

Build quality was high because the car was assembled slowly on a dedicated assembly line. Simply, the Toronado was one of the great cars of its day.

That Oldsmobile was able to overcome the inertia of General Motors to produce the front-drive Toronado was nothing short of amazing, for it was by no means a conventional car. With its hidden headlamps, sloped nose, fastback deck, neatly cropped tail, and enormous, round wheelwells, Toronado looked like it wanted to run—and it did. One hundred mph was achieved in impressive silence, and the big 425-cid V-8 provided a top speed of about 135, which was very fast, particularly for a big car riding a 119-inch wheelbase. The compact drivetrain opened up more interior space, and the front drive was predictive of a GM commitment to the technology that wouldn't really take hold until the early Eighties.

Series: Eldorado		
Hardtop coupe		

Weight	Price $	Production
4500	6277	17,940

Engine

Type	V-8
Displacement (ci.)	429
Bore × stroke	4.13 × 4.00
Horsepower	340
Compression ratio	10.50:1
Fuel feed	Rochester Quadrajet 4-bbl

C adillac received a smartly handsome redesign for 1965, with crisp horizontal lines and rear fenders that culminated in what looked like fins but weren't, quite. While the standard Cadillacs of 1965–67 rode wheelbases of 129.5, 133.0, and 149.8 inches, the all-new '67 Eldorado rode on a trim 120 inches. Like the 1966–67 Olds Toronado, the Eldo was a front-driver with fine performance and startling physical presence: Despite that concise wheelbase, the car was a boggling 221 inches, nose to tail.

The open Biarritz was discontinued to make way for the new Eldo, which carried on the dictum of GM design chief Bill Mitchell that, no matter how many mechanicals might be shared by similar cars in different divisions, the styling of each would be unique. The Eldorado name had been introduced in 1953 and had maintained a devoted following ever since.

The 1967 Eldorado (hardtop only, for now) had the familiar name but was a different kind of animal. It announced itself with a dramatically vee'd eggcrate grille, hidden headlamps, ventless side glass, and a tucked-up, prowlike tail. The C-pillar was dramatically wide, and although it didn't help the driver's vision, it contributed to an overall impression of aggressive elegance. This was a Cadillac for the daughter or son of the traditional Cadillac owner.

As with Toronado, engineering was the real story here. Front drive tried to address understeer, a dubious Cadillac hallmark, and brought almost neutral handling. The "split" transmission (separate torque converter and gearbox linked by a chain drive and sprocket) was mated with the division's thumping 429-cid, 340-hp V-8. For 1968–69, the 472 stepped in to produce 375 horsepower.

Amusingly, the division leaned toward "LaSalle" as the new car's name, until seeing that a recent book labeled that long-ago companion make "Cadillac's only failure."

"Eldorado," it was, then, and emphatically so.

The '67 Eldorado was the most significant Cadillac of the Sixties. Based on the front-drive Oldsmobile Toronado, the similarly set up Eldo was a dramatic departure for Cadillac, and a bit of a marketing risk, too. Traditional Cadillac buyers skewed "older," so a coupe with razor-sharp lines might have been doomed. But nearly 18,000 were produced for the model year, and the car's success continued for decades. The Eldorado's origins date to 1959 and GM's XP-727 program that eventually led to a pair of rejected 1961 and '63 full-size clays of new Cadillacs. After some false starts that included a coffin-nosed proposal, a full-size 1964 clay called XP-825 was approved as the production Eldorado.

Series: Camaro		
Z/28 coupe		
Weight	**Price $**	**Production**
2920	3500	602
Engine		
Type	V-8	
Displacement (ci.)	302	
Bore × stroke	4.00 × 3.00	
Horsepower	290 (stated)	
Compression ratio	11.00:1	
Fuel feed	Holley 4-bbl	

C hevy's first-year Camaro turned heads when it arrived in showrooms on September 21, 1966. Like rival Ford Mustang, it could be tailored to suit the buyer's needs and temperament. Camaro offered a pair of inline sixes (194 and 230 cid) and V-8s in displacements of 302, 327, 350 and 396 cubic inches.

The Z/28 option began to roll off assembly lines at the close of 1966, with the first few cars reaching select dealerships in January 1967.

The Z/28 had the 302 V-8 (maximum displacement for Sports Car Club of America racers) and a close- or wide-ratio 4-speed gearbox. The engine was created when Chevy fitted its 327 block with the short-stroke crank from the 283 V-8. Although nominally rated at 290 horsepower, true output was higher, and a Z/28 could zip from zero to 60 in 6.7 seconds. Chevy advertising called the Z/28 "the closest thing to a 'Vette, yet."

However, wheel hop was a recurring problem on first-year V-8 Camaros, partly because both rear shocks were mounted forward of the rear axle. Things were better noseward because of a front sub-frame in combination with unit construction. In a technique that had been used on high-end European cars, the sub-frame was isolated from the body by rubber inserts that Camaro engineers referred to as "biscuits."

Braking was state of the art for the day, with power front discs and metallic-lined rear drums. The Z ran 15×6 Corvette wheels mounting 7.75×15 tires.

Because of its weight-to-power ratio, the 302 was widely campaigned by Chevrolet and independent race teams, and performed well against similarly equipped Mustangs and other competitors.

Only 602 Z/28s were produced for the model year.

Chevy's brand new Camaro arrived in showrooms on September 21, 1966. Because Corvair, a companion model, had been forced to carry on without its popular turbo unit, the marque positioned Camaro as its affordable performance player. Although the Z/28 was top dog right from the jump, the badging did not appear on the car until 1968. Zs from 1967, then, are virtually impossible to differentiate from standard coupes—much to the rue of careless stoplight racers driving something other than a Camaro. The Z/28 was a fearsome competitor on the Trans Am race circuit, and in fact abruptly ended Mustang's dominance of those races, rekindling interest in the whole series.

Series: Impala SS		
SS coupe		
SS convertible		
Weight	**Price $**	**Production**
3615	3003	2124
3650	3254	(427-cid total)

Engine

Type	V-8
Displacement (ci.)	427
Bore × stroke	4.25 × 3.75
Horsepower	385
Compression ratio	10.25:1
Fuel feed	Holley 4-bbl

Classic muscle cars of the Sixties rode midsize platforms, and yet many drivers found the siren song of full-size screamers irresistible. Chevy's Impala SS, in its final year as a separate series for 1967, was again available in just two trims: a two-door hardtop and a two-door convertible. In that, SS was distinguished from the related Impala, Bel Air, Biscayne, and Caprice, each of which could be had in a multitude of body styles, including station wagons.

Something else distinguished the '67 SS, too: availability of Chevy's fine new-for-'66 big-block 427 V-8, which produced a neck-snapping 385 horse-power. The motor was essentially a 396, with that engine's stroke and an enlarged bore.

A domed hood with three simulated air intakes was unique to the Impala SS 427; likewise a heavy-duty suspension and front stabilizer bar.

The Impala SS 427 had unique crossed-flags "427" badging. A badge with crossed flags above "427 TURBO-JET" indicated any full-size Chevy *other than the Impala* SS 427 that had been fitted with the big-block. The "SS" logo appeared only on the grille and on the panel separating the taillights.

The lower body of the Impala SS 427 was finished in narrow black all the way to the rear quarter panels.

The big Impala was fast and handled pretty well, despite 3500–3650 pounds of beef and a considerable rear overhang. Typical of the era, brake fade was a problem in hard applications.

A 3.07:1 axle ratio and Positraction couldn't eliminate wheel spin that was a problem from a dead stop. A higher axle ratio, 3.73:1, was available, as well as a Muncie M-20 four-speed manual transmission.

Model-year production of the Impala SS 427 was a modest 2,124.

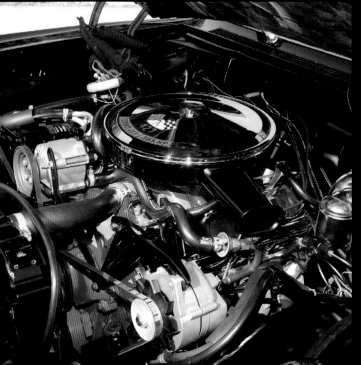

Performance Chevys for 1967 included hot rod versions of Camaro, Chevy II, and Chevelle, but none of those were as imposing as the Impala SS 427, offered as a hardtop or convertible coupe. Like stablemates Biscayne, Bel Air, and Caprice, the Impala was built on Chevy's full-size chassis, with a 119-inch wheelbase. In this, the Impala SS (in its last year as a separate series) was rather in the mold of the Pontiac Catalina 2+2, another big, powerful coupe. SS Impala interiors were all-vinyl (a presumed step up from cloth), with Strato front buckets, center console, and floor shift. A Strato bench with column shift was a no-cost option.

Series: Cougar		
Hardtop coupe		
GT hardtop coupe		
XR-7 hardtop coupe		
Weight	**Price $**	**Production**
2988	2851	116,260
3000	3175	7412
3015	3081	27,221
Engine		
Type	V-8	
	V-8	
	V-8	
Displacement (ci.)	289	
	289	
	390	
Bore × stroke	4.00 × 2.87	
	4.00 × 2.87	
	4.05 × 3.78	
Horsepower	200	
	225	
	320	
Compression ratio	9.30:1	
	9.30:1	
	10.50:1	
Fuel feed	2-bbl carburetor	
	4-bbl carburetor	
	4-bbl carburetor	

The '67 Cougar was critical to Mercury's determined trek back to "performance car" status. Big and boatlike throughout much of the Fifties, and the same in the early Sixties—with the exception of the modestly powered compact Comet—Merc needed a performance-and-image transfusion.

The new-for-'67 Cougar addressed the nameplate's needs by taking a page from FoMoCo's own Mustang. Although some 400 pounds heavier than the 1967–68 Mustangs, Cougar showed similar long-hood/short-deck proportions. But unlike Mustang, the first-generation Cougar offered V-8 engines only, no sixes.

The entry-level engine was a 289 producing 200 horsepower with a two-barrel carburetor or 225 with a four barrel. Also available was a 390 with 320 horsepower. A 427 (390 hp) and a 428 (335 hp) were added for 1968, as well as a 302 in 210- and 230-hp variations.

Three trim levels of Cougar were offered: base, GT, and XR-7. The GT was the mover, as it came with the 390, power front-disc brakes, low-restriction exhaust system, and stiffened suspension. A limited-slip rear axle was also available.

XR-7 was the luxury Cougar, with leather upholstery and comprehensive instrumentation set in a *faux* walnut dash. The XR-7 came standard with a four-speed manual; an alternative was the Merc-O-Matic Select Shift automatic.

Visible changes for '68 were minor, the most prominent being federally mandated side-marker lights. The model year also brought the GT-E, which ran with the 427.

Tuning specialist Bud Moore (working with Dan Gurney, Parnelli Jones, Peter Revson, and Ed Leslie), campaigned 1967 Cougars in the Sports Car Club of America's Trans Am series. At the end of the season, Cougar finished a close second to its corporate sibling, Ford Mustang, but ahead of Chevrolet Camaro. Cougar withdrew from Trans Am racing after only one season.

Following Cougar's September 1966 debut, *Road & Track* magazine offered a nicely understated and very true sentiment: "In its standard form, the Cougar can be described as a Mustang shell with longer more expensive-looking sheet metal, suspension refinements that make it ride somewhat more like a Thunderbird, and certain things that one expects on certain cars, like disappearing headlights." Television radio, and magazine ads anointed Cougar "the man's car," which is so presumptuous that it's a surprise that many women liked and purchased Cougars. Other adverts proclaimed, "America's first luxury sports car at a popular price"and gave a special nod to the car's exotic name: "Untamed Elegance." If all of that sounds like more than any one car could (or should) deliver, it probably was, but Cougar was capable and appealing. Like Mustang, it could be had with a plethora of options

Series: GTO		
Coupe		
Hardtop coupe		
Convertible		

Weight	Price $	Production
3425	2871	7029
3430	2935	65,176
3515	3165	9517

Engine	
Type	V-8
	HO V-8
Displacement (ci.)	400
Bore × stroke	4.12 × 3.75
Horsepower	335
	360
Compression ratio	10.75:1
Fuel feed	Rochester 4-bbl

Details can mean so much. To their muscle car's pleasing nose, Pontiac designers added simple polished "chain link" grille inserts. At the tail, they resculpted some edges and cleaned up the lamps. Without disturbing the matchless lines of the '66, the stylists had created an aesthetic triumph—the 1967 GTO.

There was something fresh behind that gorgeous new grille: The standard engine was now a 400-cid enlargement of the 389-cid V-8. Compression was unchanged and the base four-barrel again made 335 bhp. But taking over the 360-bhp slot from the discontinued tri-carb setup was a new four-barrel High Output option. It cost $77 extra and added a higher-lift cam, free-flow exhaust manifolds, and an open-element air cleaner.

For another $263, the HO mill could be fitted with Ram Air. These ultimate GTO V-8s had extra-strong valve springs, a longer-duration cam, and were underrated at 360 bhp. The Ram Air package consisted of hardware that opened the otherwise nonfunctional hood scoops, plus a pan that went around the open-element air cleaner and mated to the hood with a foam-rubber skirt. Ram Air was a factory option ordered for 751 cars, but the pan and scoop parts were shipped in the trunk of the car for installation by the dealer. The owner was advised to refit the closed-scoop hardware during wet weather.

Hurst-shifted three- and four-speeds were the manual transmission offerings. Ram Air versions could use stick or automatic, but the 4.33:1 axle ratio was mandatory. Replacing the two-speed automatic was the three-speed Turbo Hydra-matic. When it was ordered with a center console, the gear lever was relocated from the steering column to the floor and a Hurst Dual Gate shifter was used. The driver could leave the lever in Drive, or slide it into an adjacent gate for fully manual shifting.

Among other new options were power front disc brakes ($105) and a hood-mounted tach ($84).

Detail revisions fine-tuned the GTO's styling, while underhood, a 400-cid V-8 replaced the hallowed 389. Of 81,722 GTOs built for '67, this is one of 13,827 equipped with the 360-bhp High Output engine. The GTO's cabin was still top-flight, even if the dash did trade wood trim for a woodgrain vinyl appliqué.

Series: GT500		
Fastback coupe		
Weight	**Price $**	**Production**
3000	4195	2050
Engine		
Type	V-8	
Displacement (ci.)	428	
	427	
Bore × stroke	4.13 × 3.98	
	4.23 × 3.78	
Horsepower	335 (stated)	
	410/425	
Compression ratio	10.50:1	
	11.00:1	
Fuel feed	two Holley 4-bbl	
	two Holley 4-bbl	

T he first Ford Mustangs went on sale in mid-April 1964, as 1965 models. Approximately 677,000 Mustangs were produced that first year, vindicating Ford's "something for everyone" approach that was achieved via a staggering list of options. The performance Mustang was the GT, most of which had the 225-horsepower 289 V-8 with four-barrel carb and a three-speed, fully synchronized stick shift.

Even more performance followed. Texan Carroll Shelby burst onto the racing scene in the mid-Fifties with a race-modified 1949 MG TC. The Mustang was a natural car for Shelby to tinker with (he had already stuffed Ford 289 V-8s into AC Ace roadsters to create the Cobra), and his first offering, the '65 Shelby GT350, was glorious. Ford's days of getting its clock cleaned in SCCA competition by Corvettes were about to end, as every race-version 350 had a 289 goosed to 290 hp via a wilder camshaft profile and many other mods, plus a unique rear axle, suspension, and steering box, and functional rear brake vents.

Buoyed by the SCCA success of his GT350, Shelby added a more intimidating ride for 1967, the GT500. While the GT350 carried on with the 289, the 500 soared with Ford's new 428-cid V-8, developing a claimed 335 horsepower, though 400–410 was more like it. (Like other automakers, Ford wished to keep insurance companies in the dark about the actual power of its most muscular machinery.) The intake manifold from Ford's 427 and twin Holley four-barrel carbs helped reach max horsepower. Thus equipped, a GT500 ran from zero to 60 in 6.5 to 7.2 seconds.

Those figures were good but not great, so Shelby installed Ford's more familiar 427 big-block into a very small number of 500s. Introduced as a production engine in 1963, the motor cranked out 410 or 425 hp and made these GT500s race-ready.

A few '67 GT500s ran with Ford's powerful and coarse 427 V-8, but that engine made the car nose-heavy. Ford's 428 "Police Interceptor" eliminated that problem and was more refined, as well. The engine had been developed with hydraulic lifters (rather than mechanical ones) to give smooth power to full-size cars, such as the '66 Galaxie 500 7.0 Litre. The 428 could be put together on standard assembly lines, with less-exacting tolerances than those required for the raucous, race-bred 427. When it became available for Mustang, the 428 completely changed the dynamics of the street. Here was a motor that didn't mind city traffic, but that gave potent performance when asked.

Series: AMX		
2-seat fastback coupe		
Weight	**Price $**	**Production**
3097	3245	6725
Engine		
Type	V-8	
	V-8	
	V-8	
Displacement (ci.)	290	
	343	
	390	
Bore × stroke	3.75 × 3.28	
	4.08 × 3.28	
	4.17 × 3.57	
Horsepower	225	
	280	
	315	
Compression ratio	10.00:1	
	10.20:1	
	10.20:1	
Fuel feed	4-bbl carburetor	
	4-bbl carburetor	
	4-bbl carburetor	

A s the Big Three soared during the Performance Era, comparatively tiny American Motors decided it would not be left in the metaphoric or literal dust. Hence the 1968 AMX—essentially AMC's performance-oriented Javelin ponycar shortened by 12 inches, to ride on a very trim 97-inch wheelbase with one's choice of three able V-8s.

AMX was born because company chairman Roy Chapin Jr. wanted to demonstrate that AMC was capable of more than the workaday Rambler, and because design chief Dick Teague had a powerful fondness for two-seaters. Among four show cars developed by Teague, at Chapin's urging, for showing in late 1965 was a rumble-seat novelty that Teague called AMX (for "American Motors Experimental").

Teague and the rest of AMC busily prepared Javelin for a 1967 introduction, and the two-seat AMX (sans rumble seats) was ready the following year. Although the new car was clearly sourced from Javelin, it had a more dramatic fastback roofline, a unique grille, and emphatic sheet metal creases that swept aft from the leading edge of the rear wheel wells. Although AMX did well against Corvette in SCCA events, AMC never called it a "sports car."

A 290-cid V-8 produced 225 horsepower. For real oomph, buyers could select a 280-horse 343 or a 315-hp 390. With the last, an AMX could speed from zero to 60 mph in 6.7 seconds and top out at 130.

Production was 6725 for 1968 and 8293 for the unchanged 1969 edition. AMX managed 4116 units for 1970, and then was allowed to expire.

The AMX/3, of which six were built in 1970, was a mid-engine idea that might have been the next generation AMX, but by the turn of the new decade, AMC lacked the resources to pursue such esoterica—and a shame it is, too.

People who purchased a '68 AMX went most often with the 315-horsepower 390 V-8. The 390 shared the heads of the 280-hp 343 but had its own block, which had larger bearings and a crankshaft and connecting rods that were forged instead of cast. All AMX motors used a single four-barrel carburetor. A Borg-Warner four-speed was standard; a three-speed automatic with floor shift was optional. Factory axle ratios ranged from 2.87:1 to 3.54:1, with dealer-installed 4.10:1 and 5.00:1 gears available. Underneath was a heavy-duty suspension, E70×14 tires, a beefy front sway bar, and a pair of trailing arms that acted like traction bars to fight rear-axle power hop. Although an AMX couldn't stay with a Corvette in the curves, it was otherwise one of the best-handling domestic cars of its day.

Series: Sting Ray		
Coupe		
Convertible roadster		
Weight	**Price $**	**Production**
3055	4663	9936
3065	4320	18,630
Engine		
Type	V-8	
Displacement (ci.)	327	
	427	
Bore × stroke	4.00 × 3.25	
	4.25 × 3.76	
Horsepower	300/350	
	390/400/435	
Compression ratio	10.00:1	
Fuel feed	Rochester 4MV 4-bbl	
	three Rochester 2-bbl	

orvette fanciers remain split over the aesthetics and other attributes of the third-generation (C3) Corvette, the aggressively shovel-nosed car that came to be called the "Shark." Handsome on its own terms for debut-year 1968, the car suffered because of inevitable comparisons to the peerless Sting Rays of Corvette's second generation.

The basis of the 1968 Corvette body was the Mako Shark II show car, which not only put an end to early speculation about a new mid-engine Corvette but abandoned the vaguely European styling of the pervious generation in favor of an aggressively macho, very American design that, in retrospect anyway, suggests a pugnacious Camaro.

The new car had noticeable kick-ups at the front and, in particular, at the rear, which imparted a blunt look that wasn't as aerodynamic as a glance might suggest.

As in 1967, top engine remained the 427, with the same maximum horsepower, 435. The big-block also was available in 390- and 400-horse iterations. A somewhat milder (and more fuel friendly) V-8 kick was provided by an available 327-cid unit, developing 300 or 350 horsepower. In 400- and 435-horse form, the 427s ran with tri-power setups, with each carb a two-barrel unit.

Those hi-po '67 Corvettes could dash from zero to 60 mph in about 5.7 seconds, and even the "lesser" engines accomplished the sprint in 7.7. That was impressive because these cars weighed 100–200 pounds more than the previous Sting Rays. Skeptics huffed that the new 'Vettes had grown lumpish and ungainly.

Ragtops outsold coupes two to one for 1967, but the following year coupes (which had removable top and back glass) won, 22,154 to 16,608.

The Stingray name returned for 1969, though now as a single word instead of two. A 350-cid V-8 came on board to replace the 327; horsepower remained at 300 or 350.

A mantra of American business goes, "You can't argue with success"—and no Corvette has been more successful than the third-generation "Shark," which prevailed for an astounding 15 model years. Total Corvette production for '68 was 28,296, an increase of about 4.5 percent over 1967. Most new owners were happy, but "buff book" reviewers complained about a tricky winking dash; wipers that couldn't always clear the pop-up cowl; and inadequate cooling on big-block models. The dramatic, wasp-waisted styling meant decreased cockpit room, and there was less luggage space than before. Plus, the Shark was about 150 pounds heavier than the '67. If new owners noticed, they weren't telling their friends: Corvette sales for 1969 rose by nearly another 30 percent, to 38,762. That was success, and Chevy wasn't about to argue.

Series: Charger		
R/T hardtop coupe		
Weight	Price $	Production
3575	3506	17,665
Engine		
Type	V-8	
	Hemi V-8	
Displacement (ci.)	440	
	426	
Bore × stroke	4.32 × 3.75	
	4.25 × 3.75	
Horsepower	375	
	425	
Compression ratio	10.00:1	
	10.25:1	
Fuel feed	Carter 4-bbl	
	two Carter 4-bbl	

Charger debuted as a sharply creased 1966 fastback with striking full-width front and rear fascias and a unique full-length interior console. Production for model-year '66 was 37,344; it plummeted to 15,788 for '67. The dramatic nature of the drop helped prompt Dodge Division to re-do Charger for 1968—and in doing so, it created one of the best-liked and most iconic cars of the Muscle Era.

The top '68 was the R/T (Road/Track), which produced 375 horsepower with Dodge's 440 Magnum V-8, or a thumping 425 with the optional 426-cid Hemi. These were serious engines that delivered serious performance: 6.5 seconds zero to 60 with the 440 Magnum, and mid-five runs with the Hemi.

R/Ts equipped with the 440 topped out at better than 113 mph, while Hemi versions didn't quit until 142–156 mph.

The handsome redesign for '68 retained the previous car's hidden headlamps as well as the full-width fascias and rears. The car ran on the same 117-inch wheelbase as before. Body proportions were improved with newly rounded edges and other surfaces. The fastback roofline now had a "tunnelback" profile courtesy of an inset, vertical rear window flanked by "flying-buttress" C-pillars.

What had been suggestions of dual strakes on the '66 bodysides became pronounced for '68, and curving, upthrust front fenders gave a Coke-bottle effect that suggested forward motion.

For '69, the Charger name appeared on two special models, the smoother-lined Charger 500; and the Daytona, with an elongated nose and towering rear wing. Both were designed mainly for NASCAR competition.

In a brilliant piece of product placement, a black-on-black '68 Charger was the car that memorably chased Steve McQueen's '68 Mustang GT up, down, and around the hills of San Francisco in the 1968 film *Bullitt*.

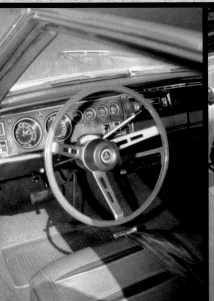

Chrysler Corporation went a little crazy with performance in the second half of the Sixties—and that was a good thing because the strategy produced some of the most capable and best-loved cars of the Muscle Era. Dodge, working off a splendid Charger platform with styling that had fallen out of favor for 1967, came up with the shapely '68, a very quick runner that was instantly popular, and that would go on to iconic status. R/T production alone approached 18,000 units, and sales of all '68 Chargers topped 92,000. When the bad guys ready their Charger for flight and buckle their lap belts in *Bullitt*, car buffs know that it's one of those no-fooling moments: The Charger was a beautiful beast.

Series: 4-4-2		
Sports coupe		
Holiday hardtop coupe		
Convertible coupe		
Weight	**Price $**	**Production**
3502	3087	4282
3512	3150	24,183
3580	3341	5142
Engine		
Type	V-8	
Displacement (ci.)	400	
Bore × stroke	4.00 × 3.98	
Horsepower	360	
Compression ratio	10.25:1	
Fuel feed	Rochester 4MV 4-bbl	

Oldsmobile's intermediate F-85/Cutlass line dumped the 115-inch wheelbase for 1968, replacing it with two new ones, at 116 and 112 inches. The 4-4-2 had been an option since 1964, but became a separate series riding on the 112-inch wheelbase for 1966. Unlike some other muscle cars, the 4-4-2 was well balanced as well as handsome, with potent power that didn't overwhelm its chassis. *Motor Trend* noted that 4-4-2s "perform, handle, and stop, without sacrificing road comfort."

For 1968, Oldsmobile's performance-oriented 4-4-2 made the leap from option package to full-fledged series. The change coincided with new Olds styling for the model year that brought an aggressive fastback roofline, a subtly aggressive bi-level hood, and a wheelbase that had been reduced by three inches, to 112. The series could be had with Olds's Holiday coupe, sports coupe, and convertible. As before, the mandatory two-door series offered a hardtop, coupe, and convertible.

When the package was introduced in calendar-year 1964 (as a '64 model), "4-4-2" indicated a four-barrel carburetor, a four-speed manual transmission, and dual exhausts. The true meaning went out the window for '65, when Olds offered an automatic transmission. Still, "4-4-2" remained synonymous with performance.

The 310 horsepower for 1964 rose to 345 for '65, and then higher still for the second-generation 4-4-2 of 1966–67, topping out at 360, which remained the maximum output for 1968–69. A forced-air induction system called W-30 Force Air, which appeared on a very few '67 Oldsmobiles, was more widely applied for '68. Intakes at the front bumper collected cold air and forced it through the carburetor, giving performance a kick in the pants. When installed in combination with a high-output cam and special heads, Force-Air boosted horsepower of the 400-cid V-8 by 10, to 360 (when running with a four-speed manual).

4-4-2's familiar heavy-duty springs and shocks, and stabilizer bars at front and rear, aided handling. The car rode on Wide-Oval F70×14 Red Line tires. Axle ratios as high as 4.46:1 could be ordered.

Inside, an optional Rally-Pac instrument cluster brought a large-dial tach and speedo, an electric clock, and a full complement of engine gauges.

The '67 4-4-2 (and the mechanically similar '68) won raves from performance enthusiasts. *Motor Trend* pulled off the 0–60 sprint in 6.7 seconds and ran the quarter in 15.3 seconds at 95 mph.

Series: Road Runner		
Coupe		
Hardtop coupe		
Weight	**Price $**	**Production**
3440	2896	29,240
3455	3034	15,359
Engine		
Type	V-8	
	Hemi V-8	
Displacement (ci.)	383	
	440	
	426	
Bore × stroke	4.25 × 3.38	
	4.32 × 3.75	
	4.25 × 3.75	
Horsepower	335	
	375	
	425	
Compression ratio	10.00:1	
	11.00:1	
	13.50:1	
Fuel feed	4-bbl carburetor	
	4-bbl carburetor	
	two 4-bbl carburetor	

When *Motor Trend* named the Plymouth Road Runner its 1969 Car of the Year, the editors cited the new budget muscle car's allure as an affordable midsize two-door coupe that gave very strong yet well-mannered performance, good braking, and clean, simple styling.

Simplicity may be, in fact, the overarching theme of Road Runner. In base form, it was very nearly a stripper—a car without much in the way of creature comforts (not even bucket seats), but with a dedicated focus on speed. And at $2896, it was Chrysler-Plymouth's calculated attempt to put young buyers into its cars. Offered as a coupe and hardtop coupe for 1968, and joined by a convertible for '69, the Road Runner line had combined 1968 production of 44,779 and, for '69, a sterling 84,420.

The pillared coupes were about $150 cheaper than the hardtops, so they outsold the hardtops, though the latter were outwardly more stylish. But whatever the body style, a Road Runner with the entry-level Super Commando 383-cid, 335-horse V-8 wasn't to be trifled with. That, plus a stiffened suspension and a durable A833 four-speed manual, suggested an all-business attitude.

The available Super Commando 440 pushed out 375 or 390 horses for 1969, but the killer was the 426-cid Hemi, available for an extra $800 and rated at 425 hp (though actual output was far higher). In that trim, a Road Runner could top 120 mph flat out and fly from zero to 60 in as few as 5.5 seconds. An experienced driver could pilot a Hemi RR with a 4.10:1 rear-axle ratio through the quarter in 13.5 seconds at 105 mph.

Plymouth paid Warner Bros. $50,000 for the Road Runner name, and for a horn that, yes, went "Beep Beep!" But in every other way, the car was dead serious.

Simultaneously whimsical (*Beep! Beep!*) and dead serious (as in: "Check out my rapidly diminishing taillights."), the '68 Road Runner was a fascinating combination of practicality, speed, and marketing genius. It rode Chrysler's B-body, specifically the plain-Jane Belvedere body. Road Runner came to market largely without amenities—without much of anything except a reasonably lightweight midsize body and a ferocious performance package. And a sub-$3000 price calculated to attract young buyers was the tip-in. So great was the rush to get Road Runner to market that its cartoon decal was black, white, and gray for 1968; color wouldn't be added until '69.

Series: Chevelle SS 396		
Coupe		
Hardtop coupe		
Weight	**Price $**	**Production**
3165	2548	86,307
3205	2611	(all SS packages)
Engine		
Type	V-8	
Displacement (ci.)	396	
Bore × stroke	4.09 × 3.76	
Horsepower	325/350/375	
Compression ratio	11.00:1	
Fuel feed	Rochester 4-bbl	

hevy's SS 396 had been a separate model for 1968, but for '69 it became a $348 option package that expanded its availability from Malibu's sport coupe and convertible to El Camino and—most significantly—Chevelle's hardtop and pillared coupes.

In "base" form the 396-cid V-8 produced 325 horsepower. An upgraded 396 coded L34 was rated at 350 hp, but in L78 trim that figure leapt to 375, with plenty of low-end grunt.

The L78 was relatively simple engine with a solid-lifter camshaft, an 800-cfm Holley carburetor, and forged pistons.

About 400 L78/SS buyers parted with an additional $395 for the L98 option, which brought weight-saving aluminum heads.

One automatic transmission, the three-speed Turbo Hydra-Matic, was available with the SS 396; it was the first unit with the strength needed to handle the power put out by the motor. For L78/L98 drivers who preferred to shift manually, Muncie's fabled extra heavy duty, close-ratio "Rock Crusher" M-22 four-speed was available.

With an 11.0:1 compression ratio and 415 pound-feet of torque at 3600 rpm, the Chevelle SS 396, in top form, ripped though the quarter-mile in 14.5 seconds at 101 mph. On the street, 60 came up from rest in 6.5 seconds.

The package came with power front-disc brakes; new options included the tough F41 suspension and free-flow chambered exhausts. Chassis of SS 396s also had a 12-bolt rear axle and rear sway bar. Fourteen-inch rims were factory-standard, though many buyers elected to trade up to 15 inchers in order to accommodate larger radial tires that wouldn't be as easily scrubbed away by the 396's torque as the standard bias-belted rubber.

Chevelle slotted comfortably between the full-size Chevys and the junior Chevy II. Chevelle had been around since 1964 as an answer to Ford's popular midsize Fairlane. Although conventional in design, Chevelle offered nearly as much interior room as a full-size Impala, with exterior dimensions that recalled the beautifully balanced '55 Chevy. Modest but steady sales increases encouraged Chevrolet Division to give Chevelle a new 112-inch wheelbase for 1968. A year later, the car could be had with Chevy's hard-pulling 396 and top horsepower of 375. This made the Chevelle a familiar player in legal and extra-legal drag racing. Aggressive ad campaigns and competitive prices helped boost sales to the quarter-million mark for 1970.

Series: Charger		
Hardtop coupe		
Weight	Price $	Production
3740	4000	505
Engine		
Type	V-8	
	Hemi V-8	
Displacement (ci.)	440	
	426	
Bore × stroke	4.32 × 3.75	
	4.25 × 3.75	
Horsepower	375	
	425	
Compression ratio	10.00:1	
	10.25:1	
Fuel feed	Carter carburetor	
	two Holley 4-bbl	

Because neither the 1966–67 Dodge Charger, nor the redesigned 1968–69 model, had much success in NASCAR events, Dodge created the dramatically contoured Charger Daytona. Although radical, the car was made available to the public: About 505 were produced for Dodge, by Creative Industries in Detroit, to satisfy NASCAR's 500-unit requirement that would allow a car to be classed as a "production" machine. That suggests, rightly, that the Daytona's only real purpose was to win races—particularly against perennial Chrysler Corp. rival Ford.

The Daytona cost only $300 more than the Charger R/T hardtop, and Dodge ate between $1000 and $1500 on every one sold—and did so willingly.

Only 70 Daytonas were shipped with the 426-cid, 425-hp Hemi and just 20 of the Hemis had a close-ratio four-speed manual gearbox and a Hurst shifter. (A milder motor, the 375-horse 440, was also available.) At Talladega, the Daytona set a new official world's closed-lap speed record at just 200 mph.

Daytona's famous rear wing addressed the rear-end lift of the 1968–69 competition Chargers, and the car picked up a pointed, elongated snout for improved airflow. These changes added 5 mph on the track—or the length of about five football fields per lap. That was huge.

When Dodge and Ford finally met, it was at Talladega Speedway, where the faster Charger Daytona scrubbed its tires raw. In one encounter after another, Daytonas leapt ahead, only to fall back to conserve rubber.

Things improved in December 1969, when Daytonas took the measure of Fords and others to win the Texas 500. The Daytona went on to win 80 percent of its races in 1969 before bowing out of competition.

Dodge dealers took about 1200 orders for Daytonas and then were told by Dodge (in a bit of bad PR) to tell many of those customers to accept another Dodge model.

With its outrageous and completely functional rear wing, and its elongated snout (also completely functional), the Dodge Charger Daytona seemed a cartoon of a car—much more so, for instance, than the cartoon-inspired Road Runner. But on the track, Daytona was pure reality, and like a splash of ice water in the face of competitors. A shade over 500 were manufactured for general sale. Most of those went racing, of course—not least because the Daytona's skill set went underused on the street, and because it inevitably aroused the interest of John Law. So successful was the race-version Daytona that it was banned from competition after just two seasons. That was disappointing to Dodge loyalists who'd wanted more opportunities to pummel Fords and other rivals, but it was an invaluable resource for Dodge advertising, which capitalized on the "winner" mystique.

Series: Super Bee Six Pack		
Coupe		
Hardtop coupe		
Weight	**Price $**	**Production**
N/A	N/A	1907 (all)
4100	4300	
Engine		
Type	V-8	
Displacement (ci.)	440	
Bore × stroke	4.32 × 3.75	
Horsepower	390	
Compression ratio	10.50:1	
Fuel feed	three Holley 2-bbl	

n mid 1969, Chrysler engineers used some good-old hot-rodding to create one of the muscle era's most intoxicating cars.

They took Mopar's fine 375-bhp 440-cid Magnum V-8 and treated it to the time-honored hop-up of more carburetion, replacing the single Carter quad with three Holley two-barrels on an Edelbrock Hi-Riser manifold. Normal driving ran the engine on the center carb; punching it opened the two outboard Holleys and delivered an astounding 1375-cfm charge. Hemi valve springs, a hotter cam, magnafluxed connecting rods, and other fortifications helped boost output to 390 bhp.

A Hurst-shifted four-speed and a 93⁄4-inch Dana Sure-Grip diff with 4.10:1 gears were standard. TorqueFlite was optional, but disc brakes, air conditioning, and cruise control were not allowed.

Dodge's home for the new mill was the econo-muscle Coronet Super Bee, which again came with a 383-cid V-8 or the 426 Hemi. In honor of the tri-carb setup, the newcomer was called the Super Bee Six Pack, a name broadcast on the sides of one of the wilder hoods in muscledom. Its scoop lacked a filter or valve to keep out foreign elements—though it did have rain drain tubes. With its matte-black finish and NASCAR tie-down pins, the fiberglass lift-off hood said this car meant business, a message reinforced by standard steel wheels unadorned except for chrome lug nuts. (The engine and a similar hood also were offered in the '69 Plymouth Road Runner as the "440+6".)

Dodge's 440 Six Pack cost $463, about $500 less than a Hemi. No Mopar mill was as all-out fast as the Hemi. But the 440 could hang with one until 70 mph or so, and the deep-breathing Six Pack added a near-Hemi high end. "The result was a torque motor that would rev, too, a fearsome street cleaner," wrote Car and Driver's Patrick Bedard in his 1990 muscle retrospective.

With their Hemi-grade suspension, Six Pack Super Bees were surprisingly good handlers. That outrageous hood did bait cops, and made every oil check a two-person job. So what? Considering its price and performance, this Six Pack was a small-deposit, high-return steal.

Muscle got no meaner than the Super Bee Six Pack. Based on the econo-performance Coronet-derived Super Bee of '68, it got its name from the three Holley two-barrels atop its 440-cid V-8. The massive scoop was functional and the chrome pins really held down the lift-off fiberglass hood. It came without wheel covers, just chrome lug nuts. This one has optional bucket seats and console, plus the hot ticket for street work, the TorqueFlite automatic.

Series: Fairlane Cobra 428		
Hardtop coupe		
SportsRoof hardtop coupe		
Weight	**Price $**	**Production**
3490	3189	N/A
3537	3164	N/A
Engine		
Type	V-8	
Displacement (ci.)	428	
Bore × stroke	4.13 × 3.98	
Horsepower	335	
Compression ratio	10.60:1	
Fuel feed	Holley 4-bbl	

Ford jumped on the budget-muscle bandwagon in '69 with a midsize model that was a little out of character for the brand: It performed. The subject was a dressed-down Fairlane hardtop or SportsRoof fastback with the grille blacked out and minimal exterior ornamentation; about the only clue to the car's true nature were small Cobra snake emblems and "428" badges.

They signified the 428-cid Cobra Jet V-8, which was standard. The $3200 base price also included a four-speed manual, with automatic a mere $37 option. Estimates put the Cobra Jet's true output at around 400 bhp, though Ford rated it at 335. The optional Ram Air induction system cost $133 and used a functional hood scoop to feed an air-cleaner breather valve that opened under heavy throttle. These CJ-R engines retained the 335-bhp rating, but were stronger than the standard mill, and turned high-13s at 102 mph.

Like the '68 econo-racer Mopars that launched the segment, Cobra stuck to basics. A "competition" suspension with staggered rear shocks, F70x14 tires, and hood-lock pins were standard. Power steering ($100) and power front discs ($65) were extras. Limited slip was a $63 option, but available ratios included 4.30:1 gears in a bulletproof Detroit Locker, which required an engine oil cooler. Interior was bench-seat plain; bucket seats with console added $169, an 8000-rpm tach, $48.

Like the mainstream intermediate on which it was based, the Cobra had a benign feel on the road, with predictable handling and numb power steering. But unlike most Fords, it flew.

"The 428 had...a lethargic way about it: it wasn't zingy like a Chevy," recalled Patrick Bedard for a 1990 *Car and Driver* retrospective. "But it had earth-mover torque, and it stayed in tune—exactly what street racers needed. It was good with an automatic, too: just punch it and hang on. Which meant that every CJ was a threat no matter what kind of yahoo was in the chair."

Inspired by low-buck midsize muscle rivals, Ford uncoiled the Fairlane Cobra for '69. It came standard with the brawny 428-cid Cobra Jet V-8. This is the base version; the Ram Air option added a hood scoop that mated to an air-cleaner breather setup. Both were rated at 335 bhp. Fairlane Cobras also came as SportsRoof fastbacks, but the formal-roof notchbacks were about 60 pounds lighter.

Series: Mustang Boss 302

Fastback coupe

Weight	Price $	Production
3300	3588	1934

Engine

Type	V-8
Displacement (ci.)	302
Bore × stroke	4.00 × 3.00
Horsepower	290
Compression ratio	9.50:1
Fuel feed	Motorcraft 4-bbl

Series: Mustang Boss 429

Fastback coupe

Weight	Price $	Production
3870	4798	858

Engine

Type	V-8
Displacement (ci.)	429
Bore × stroke	4.36 × 3.59
Horsepower	375 (stated)
Compression ratio	10.50:1
Fuel feed	Holley 4-bbl

Ford raced small-block V-8 Mustangs in Trans-Am competition, so a street version was inevitable. The '69 Boss 302 (with the "Boss" moniker coined by designer Larry Shinoda) was hailed by many as the best Mustang yet—a beautifully balanced blend of style, road manners, and straight-line performance. Because of the relative light weight of the small-block V-8, the Boss 302 handled exceptionally well.

Only 1934 of the $3588 Boss 302s were produced for the model year, but buyers drove away with somewhat more than the stated 290 hp, a Holley 4-barrel carb, aluminum rocker covers, and low-restriction headers. Ford claimed a 0–60 time of six seconds flat, but testers found that 6.5 seconds was nearer to reality.

Ford had racing plans for another engine in 1968: a 429-cid V-8 that was set to campaign (in midsize Torinos) in NASCAR, where eligibility rules required that the motor be installed in 500 production cars. This was the genesis of the fabled Boss 429, a "semi-hemi" engine with four-bolt mains, a forged-steel crankshaft, and a Holley four-barrel. The motor was so huge that the Mustangs had to be modified for Ford by Kar Kraft of Brighton, Michigan. This meant wider spring towers, shorter upper control arms, and a lowered suspension, plus staggered shocks and a clamp-on stabilizer bar. Although claimed output was 375 hp, the true figure was significantly greater than 400. The 429 was a high-revving engine strong enough to devour the quarter mile in about 14.0 seconds at 105–110 mph.

On the street, the handling of a 429 Mustang suffered because of that heavy motor, but if you wanted to gallop from zero to 60 mph in the high sixes, you lived with it.

A thorough restyle for 1969 made Mustang longer by four inches, mostly in front overhang on an unchanged 108-inch wheelbase. The car also became lower, wider, and heavier than in '68 (by 25 to 175 pounds, depending on the model). Vents disappeared from the side glass, and a freshened black grille was dominated by revised quad headlamps and the familiar Mustang logo, now offset to the left. The sculpted, concave bodysides that had distinguished Mustang from the beginning were gone, giving a "hunky" look that was further underscored by aggressive bulges above the rear wheel arches. A pair of inline sixes carried on alongside six V-8s, including the hugely capable 302- and 429-cid units that distinguished the year's hard-charging Boss models.

Series: Talladega		
SportsRoof hardtop coupe		
Weight	**Price $**	**Production**
3775	3570	754
Engine		
Type	V-8	
Displacement (ci.)	428	
Bore × stroke	4.13 × 3.98	
Horsepower	335	
Compression ratio	10.60:1	
Fuel feed	Holley 4-bbl	

Ford spent a lot of the 1960s and early 1970s watching the taillights of quicker Mopar and GM muscle rivals. But in NASCAR, the forces from Dearborn were consistent front-runners. For '69, their new machine was so hot that even superstar Richard Petty defected from Plymouth to drive it. It was called the Talladega, after NASCAR's newest superspeedway. This was Ford's answer to Dodge's wind-tunnel wonder, the Charger 500, and as required of Dodge, Ford built street versions to qualify it for racing.

The Talladega was based on the 1969 Fairlane Cobra SportsRoof, but with some vital aerodynamic differences. The nose was tapered and stretched by five inches, and a flush-mounted grille replaced the recessed production one. The front bumper was actually a Fairlane rear bumper narrowed to fit. And the rocker panels were raised one inch so the race cars could be lowered correspondingly without violating NASCAR's ride-height requirements.

NASCAR versions ran Ford's 427-cid V-8, then switched to the Boss 429. Street Talladegas used the 335-bhp 428 Cobra Jet with a columnshift automatic. None had ram air, but all got a Drag Pack oil cooler. Cobra-issue bench-seat interiors were used.

Mercury quickly copied the formula, producing the Cyclone Spoiler II. With unique striping and a rear spoiler, street versions were flashier than Talladegas, though Mercury made the 290-bhp 351 V-8 standard.

Ford's aero warriors trounced the Charger 500, winning 30 races, including eight by Petty, and bringing Ford the '69 NASCAR title. When the King Cobra version of the redesigned '70 Torino disappointed in testing, the '69 Talladegas and Spoiler IIs were retained for NASCAR's 1970 season. Petty had been lured back to Plymouth by its radical Superbird, and the title returned to Chrysler. But Ford had produced a real winner, and by happy necessity, a unique member of the muscle fraternity.

Ford built 754 Talladegas, all in Wimbledon White, Royal Maroon, or Presidential Blue. Fairlane-Cobra-issue bench-seat interiors were spartan, though power steering and brakes were standard. A single-speaker AM radio was a $61.40 option. Street Talladegas were offered for 1969 only; their racing counterparts ran in both the '69 and '70 NASCAR seasons.

Series: Firebird		
Hardtop coupe		
Convertible coupe		
Weight	**Price $**	**Production**
3080	2821	689
3330	3045	8
Engine		
Type	V-8	
Displacement (ci.)	400	
Bore × stroke	4.12 × 3.75	
Horsepower	335/345 (Ram Air)	
Compression ratio	10.75:1	
Fuel feed	4-bbl carburetor	

The '69 Trans Am is marked by ironies. Pontiac desperately wanted a competition-approved small-block V-8 engine (305 cid, max) like the 302-cube units fielded by Chevy and Ford in SCCA contests. Pontiac never got an engine of that sort during the muscle car era, but the Trans Am (a late-1969, $725 option package for the Firebird 400) carried the name of that fabled racing series.

An even greater irony is that, earlier in the Sixties, Pontiac was developing a 303-cid V-8, a downsized version of their own 326/389, with unique tunnel-port heads. But the effort went nowhere, and the division wouldn't have a V-8 engine in the 302-cid neighborhood until an anemic, 135-hp 301 V-8, which was offered for 1977, by which time performance was a dead issue in Detroit.

Pontiac's interest in performance and sophisticated suspensions got a good airing with the Pontiac Firebird Sprint Turismo (PFST) of 1968. The car was a one-off based on the everyday '68 Firebird, but riding very low on a stiffened suspension. Power came from a 400-cid Ram-Air V-8 developing 335 horsepower with a three-speed Turbo Hydra-Matic. All that oomph was delivered to the pavement with help from a 3.55 rear axle and a limited-slip differential. Among the other add-ons were wider rims and wheels, a hood-mounted tach, and functional hood and bodyside scoops.

Key elements of the PFST were adapted for production, notably the stiffened suspension and the 335/345-hp 400. Three- and four-speed manuals joined the Hydra-Matic unit.

Total cost was about $4500—pricey but still a good deal considering that the Trans Am ripped from zero to 60 mph in 5.0 seconds.

In another irony, Pontiac's first inclination was to call the car Formula or Sebring. Well, Sebring went to Plymouth, of course, and Pontiac had its own future plans for Formula.

For 1969, the Firebird was redesigned below the beltline (less rounded wheel openings were one marker) and picked up a host of federally mandated safety features, including security lockouts for ignition, steering, and gearshift. The Trans Am never competed in the series of the same name, but it invariably gave a good account of itself on the roads, thanks to a stiffened chassis and superb brakes. Trans Am production for the '69 model year amounted to fewer than 700, including just eight convertibles and only nine cars with the optional 345-horsepower Ram Air IV engine. If you wanted a body other than white with blue stripes, you were out of luck; the only color choices were on the interiors. Gold upholstery trim was one available, but seldom-ordered, option.

Series: GTO		
Hardtop coupe		
Convertible coupe		
Weight	**Price $**	**Production**
3503	3510	6725
3553	3736	108
Engine		
Type	V-8 HO	
Displacement (ci.)	400	
Bore × stroke	4.12 × 3.75	
Horsepower	366/370 (stated)	
Compression ratio	10.75:1	
Fuel feed	Rochester Quadrajet 4-bbl	

A bold redesign of the GTO for 1968 brought bulged bodysides, a steeply raked hardtop roofline, and a dominant bumper/grille assembly with new hidden headlamps. The car's nose was body-colored Endura plastic that wouldn't easily chip or dent.

The wheelbases of all '68 GM intermediate two-doors slimmed by three inches, to 112, and although a new full-perimeter frame added about 75 pounds to what GTO carried for 1967, it also improved rigidity and handling. Four-hundred-cid V-8s continued, though with a new 350-horse base unit. Complete horsepower ratings for 1968 were 265/350/360. With the top engine, a '68 Goat could clock 6.5 seconds zero to 60–quick, but not as quick as a 428 Cobra Jet Ford Torino or a Hemi-equipped Chrysler product.

For 1969, Pontiac introduced a $354 option package for GTO hardtops and convertibles called The Judge (as in, "Here come da Judge!"), which came with a new, 366-horse Ram-Air III version of the 400. Another new variant of the 400, which was available with all GTOs for '69, was a Ram-Air IV setup, with grille intakes, that cranked out 370 horsepower.

Late in the '69 model year, a 370-horse Ram-Air V sneaked onto the "available" list; with either of the 370-hp engines, The Judge ran the quarter in 14–14.5 seconds at about 100 mph. Zero to 60 was accomplished in 6.2 seconds.

The first 500 Judges were an orange shade called Carousel Red. The "Judge" name was announced in psychedelic lettering via front-fender decals.

Despite its outré looks, The Judge was a legit street machine that, rather unaccountably, went virtually ignored in the marketplace. Only 6725 hardtops were produced, and a puny 108 convertibles. Potential buyers missed a bet in that debut year because in the great 1971 movie *Two-Lane Blacktop*, actor Warren Oates, driving a '70 GTO, elevated The Judge into legend.

In the movie *Two-Lane Blacktop*, Warren Oates slows his new '70 GTO Judge in order to pick up a very young chick who's hitchhiking. It's obvious that Oates is fortyish, arguably too old to own a Judge, and certainly too old to fool with a teenage stranger. But the Judge, with its top horsepower purposely understated at 370, was a paradox: a smartly styled hardtop coupe that might pass for "respectable" (if nobody noticed the "Judge" fender decal) but one that was all about brute force inside the cockpit and under the hood. "Here come da Judge" might have been more usefully translated as "Dere *go* da Judge!"

Series: GSX		
Hardtop coupe		
Weight	Price $	Production
4000	5100	678

Engine

Type	V-8
Displacement (ci.)	455
Bore × stroke	4.31 × 3.90
Horsepower	360
Compression ratio	10.50:1
Fuel feed	Rochester 4-bbl

eneral Motors surrendered itself to temptation in 1970 and lifted its 400-cid limit on intermediate cars. That unleashed some of the quickest automobiles ever to come out of Detroit and helped make this the pinnacle year for American muscle.

At the forefront of the rush to power was none other than Buick. Its performance offering was again based on the midsize Skylark, which got fresh styling that added two inches of body length on an unchanged wheelbase for '70. Replacing the GS 400 and its 400-cid V-8 was the GS 455, named for its new 455-cid V-8. The new mill offered not only advantages of displacement, but had bigger valves, better heads, and a hotter camshaft. It was rated at 350 bhp. Its prodigious 510 lb-ft of torque (at a subterranean 2800 rpm) was exceeded among production cars only by Cadillac's 472- and 500-cid V-8s. Standard on GS models were functional hood scoops that mated to dual air-cleaner intakes. For the really power hungry, Buick offered the 455 Stage I performance package. Its tweaks included a hotter cam, even larger valves with stronger springs, ported heads, and revised carburetor jetting. Torque was unchanged, and Buick slyly put horsepower at 360, but most testers said it was over 400. A bargain at just $199, the Stage I package included a Positraction 3.64:1 axle and performance modifications to the available manual and automatic transmissions.

During the model year, Buick unveiled the ultimate expression of its ultimate supercar, the GSX. It added $1196 to the GS 455 and came in either Apollo White or Saturn Yellow set off by unique stripes and spoilers. A hood-mounted tach, Hurst-shifted four-speed, Polyglas G60x15s on seven-inch-wide wheels, front discs, and heavy-duty suspension were included. Of 678 GSXs built, 488 were ordered with the Stage 1 upgrade, which cost $113 on a GSX. A 13.38-second pass at 105.5 mph prompted *Motor Trend* to crown the GS 455 Stage 1 "the quickest American production car we had ever tested." Most other magazines were in the high 13s. Any way you cut it, Buick had earned its place on muscle's all-time, all-star team.

Buick's restyled Skylark hosted the GS 455, so named for its new 455-cid V-8. Stage 1 upgrades gave it 360 bhp. The midyear GSX option elevated the GS 455's profile with an exclusive package of aero aids and graphics, creating one of the muscle era's great cars. Functional hood scoops fed standard ram air induction; note the hood-mounted tach.

Series: Camaro		
Sport coupe		
Z28 sport coupe		
Weight	**Price $**	**Production**
3190	2839	124,889
3190	3412	8733

Engine	
Type	V-8
Displacement (ci.)	350
Bore × stroke	4.00 × 3.48
Horsepower	300/360
Compression ratio	11.00:1
Fuel feed	Holley 4-bbl

The aggressively handsome 1970 Camaro retained the 108-inch wheelbase of its first-generation predecessor but didn't share a single body panel. The unified, long-hood/short-deck body, fronted by an aggressively outthrust nose, excited buyers and helped kill the pain caused by the deletion of a convertible.

The model year brought a few firsts for Camaro: rearview mirror glued to the windshield; side-impact door beams; in-glass antenna; and concealed windshield wipers (optional). Instruments, even optional ones, now were grouped together in the main pod; none were at the console.

'70 Camaros ordered with the RS package came with Euro-style parking lamps that sat level with the headlights above abbreviated, bladelike bumperettes; no bumper crosses the RS grille. Buyers who combined the RS with the SS option drove off with a 350-cid V-8 rated at 300 horsepower. The three-piece spoiler devised by Hurst was an option that would become standard for model-year 1971.

At $573, Camaro's 1970 Z28 package wasn't inexpensive, but by any judgment it was a high-performance bargain. The standard Z28 engine no longer was the fine 302, but Chevy's LT-1 350, rated for the Z at a thumping 360 horsepower. The engine was as sophisticated as it was potent, with solid lifters, a hot cam, aluminum pistons, oversized valves, and a 780-cfm Holley four-barrel carburetor. Compression was 11.0:1. So-called "mandatory extras" were a Muncie four-speed manual transmission with Hurst shifter ($206) and Positraction ($44) with 3.73:1 gearing (a 4.10:1 gear set also was available). The new motor produced enough low-end torque for Z28 to offer its first-ever automatic transmission option, the Turbo 400.

Because the new Camaro wasn't ready for its public introduction until February 1970, only 124,889 were produced for the model year. Of that number, a mere 8733 were optioned as Z28s.

The three-piece spoiler seen on the '70 Camaro was designed by Hurst as an optional feature, which, for 1971, became standard. No Camaro convertible was offered for '70, but Hurst was contracted to build three examples of a Z28 Sunshine Special sunroof coupe. Based on the RS and toned a lively yellow with wide, black rally stripes, each Sunshine Special had a T-handle shifter in a slotted gate and a special canvas roof insert that cranked into the headliner, accordion-like, to let the sun in. The mechanism was never mass produced for Camaro, but it was adopted for Chevy's Nova in 1972 and called the Skyroof.

Series: Chevelle SS 454		
Hardtop coupe		
Convertible		
Weight	**Price $**	**Production**
4000	4930	4475 (all)
N/A	N/A	
Engine		
Type	V-8	
Displacement (ci.)	454	
Bore × stroke	4.25 × 4.00	
Horsepower	450	
Compression ratio	11.25:1	
Fuel feed	Holley 4-bbl	

The age of muscle peaked in 1970 and Chevelle was there to herald its ascent. When GM lifted its displacement ban on midsize cars, Pontiac, Olds, and Buick responded with 455-cid mills with up to 370 bhp. Chevy's retort was a 454-cid V-8 that started at 360 bhp and ended at a barbaric 450. This was muscle's summit.

The wrapper was a restyled Chevelle that again presented the Super Sport as an option package for hardtops and convertibles. As the SS 396, it cost $446 and came with a 350-bhp 402-cid V-8, power front discs, F41 suspension, Polyglas F70x14s, and a domed hood. Fat dorsal stripes were optional, but were included with the new $147 cowl-induction hood, which had a flapper near the base of the windshield that opened at full throttle to feed air to the engine.

The new SS 454 package cost $503 and included a 360-bhp hydraulic-lifter 454 called the LS5. Then there was the LS6. This was the take-no-prisoners 454, with a 800-cfm Holley four-barrel on an aluminum manifold, 11.25:1 compression, solid lifters, four-bolt mains, forged steel crank and connecting rods, forged aluminum pistons, and deep-groove accessory pullies. No production engine of the muscle car era ever had a higher factory horsepower rating. With mandatory options—including either the Rock Crusher four-speed or special Turbo 400 automatic—total cost for an LS6 was more than $1000. Axles ranged from 3.31:1 to 4.10:1, with Positraction a $42 extra.

The SS Chevelle had a handsome new dash, and on the road, exhibited far more poise than its weight and size would suggest. But the LS6 made it a superstar. Sub-14-second ETs at over 100 mph were routine.

But the LS6's thunder also seemed to signal an approaching storm, one that would dampen muscle for years to come. Testers sensed it. "Without even raising the specters of insurance and social justice," said *Car Life* after an LS6 experience, "it's fair to say that the Supercar as we know it may have gone as far as it's going."

1970 CHEVROLET CHEVELLE SS 454

The 1970 Super Sport Chevelle with the solid-lifter LS6 454-cid V-8 was a tyrannical muscle car with an unsurpassed 450-bhp factory rating. It had a restyled body and shared its new gauge cluster with the Monte Carlo. Options on this car include bucket seats and console. It also has the new cowl-induction hood, which drew air from the base of the windshield via a vacuum-controlled flapper. Of 62,372 Super Sport Chevelles and El Caminos built for '70, 4298 had the LS5 454 and 4475 had the LS6. America would not see their likes again.

Series: Challenger R/T		
Hardtop coupe		
Convertible coupe		
S.E hardtop coupe		
Weight	**Price $**	**Production**
3405	3226	14,889
3470	3535	1070
3440	3498	3979
Engine		
Type	V-8	
	Magnum V-8	
	Tri-Carb V-8	
	Hemi V-8	
Displacement (ci.)	383	
	440	
	440	
	426	
Bore × stroke	4.25 × 3.38	
	4.32 × 3.75	
	4.32 × 3.75	
	4.32 × 3.75	
Horsepower	335	
	375	
	390	
	425	
Compression ratio	9.50:1	
	10.00:1	
	10.28:1	
	10.28:1	
Fuel feed	Holley 4-bbl	
	Carter 4-bbl	
	three Carter 2-bbl	
	two Carter 4-bbl	

I f the heart and soul of a muscle car is its engine, then the '70 Challenger R/T—running with a 440-cid V-8 producing 375 horsepower—was a champ.

For 1964, Chrysler Corp fielded the all-new Plymouth Barracuda as a mild (and mainly accidental) retort to Mustang, but Dodge needed six years to mount a challenge to Ford's runaway sporty car. By the time Challenger came along, the ponycar segment was well established. But to its credit, Challenger had a hunkier, meaner look than Mustang and Camaro, and because it rode a stretched version of the Barracuda's unibody platform, it had a 110-inch wheelbase (Barracuda had 108) that made backseat living almost bearable.

Challenger was available as a hardtop and convertible, with two performance versions wearing the R/T label. The standard R/T was powered by a 335-hp 383. Step up in class and you looked at two 440s: a four-barrel Magnum with 375 horses and a Six Pack carb setup (triple two-barrels) that produced 390 hp.

The Challenger motor on the mythic mountaintop was a 426-cid Hemi cranking an eye-opening 425 hp. This engine was a $1228 option that required heavy-duty equipment.

Chrysler's TorqueFlite automatic came standard with the 440s and the Hemi. Order a manual and you got a Hurst unit with pistol-grip shifter and a Dana 60 axle. Gear ratio with the four-speed was 4.10:1, as opposed to the automatic's 3.23:1. Limited-slip differential was an extra-cost item.

An appealing cosmetic package, the SE R/T, came with leather seats and a vinyl roof.

Hemis were quickest, but not so much quicker than the 440s to justify the added cost. R/T performance with the 440 Six Pack was plenty fierce: zero to 60 mph in 6.2 seconds and blazing, 13.7-second runs through the quarter at 105 mph.

As is often the case, practical considerations suffered for the sake of design. The Challenger gave poor outward visibility, and although road manners were composed, the car felt bulky for its size.

Over and over in the allegorical 1971 road movie *Vanishing Point*, macadam-level camera setups wait for the protagonist's '70 Challenger to roar to—and past—the audience's point of view. These are stirring moments involving a frankly thrilling car that waited for buyers at their local Dodge dealer. Speed fans never had it so good. Consider that Challenger R/T's "weak-sister" horsepower rating was a robust 335, and that top output was a staggering 425. A Challenger driven by Sam Posey finished fourth in points in the 1970 Trans-Am race series. More than 30 years after *Vanishing Point*, another movie, Quentin Tarantino's *Death Proof*, featured another '70 Challenger. Was the car still awesome? Is "Dodge" spelled with a "D"?

Series: Torino Cobra		
SportsRoof hardtop coupe		
Weight	**Price $**	**Production**
4000	4200	7675
Engine		
Type	V-8	
Displacement (ci.)	429	
Bore × stroke	4.36 × 3.59	
Horsepower	370	
Compression ratio	11.30:1	
Fuel feed	Holley 4-bbl	

J udging from their newfound plumpness, Detroit's 1970 crop of intermediates were not only midsized, but middle- aged. Nowhere was that truer than at Ford, where the Torino gained an inch of wheelbase and five full inches of length, making it among the very largest cars in the segment. At least the reshaped sheetmetal looked aero-inspired, while a two-inch increase in tread width allowed Ford to squeeze in a new high-performance engine.

Replacing the willing but aged 428-cid V-8 was a new 429-cid mill. This was not the semi-hemi Boss 429 engine, but a fresh design with thin-wall construction and canted-valve heads. Ford retained a familiar moniker for the hottest versions, and built a new muscle car around them: the Torino Cobra. This was basically a SportsRoof Torino GT in fighting trim, with exposed headlamps, blackout hood, and available muscle-car touches like rear-window slats and fat Polyglas F60x15s on seven-inch-wide Magnum 500 wheels. Standard equipment included a Hurst-shifted four-speed, competition suspension with staggered rear shocks, and Cobra insignia.

The standard engine was a 10.5:1-compression 360-bhp version of the 429. Things quickly got serious with the 370-bhp Cobra variant, which had an 11.3:1 squeeze, different heads, a high-lift cam, and a 700-cfm Holley four-barrel on a high-rise manifold. With the available shaker scoop, this engine was called the 429 Cobra Jet Ram-Air, but stayed at 370 bhp. Ordering the Drag Pack with the Cobra engine added Traction-Lok 3.91:1 or Detroit Locker 4.30:1 gears, a mechanical-lifter cam, oil cooler, forged aluminum pistons, four-bolt mains, and a 780-cfm four-barrel, for a 375-bhp rating. (Early '70 ads also listed the genuine Boss 429 as a Torino Cobra option, though few were installed.)

Torino Cobras weren't as brutally overpowering as some rival big-blocks, but they were strong enough on the street. Part of the car's heft actually helped performance: With so much weight in the tail, dig off the line was excellent and its 0-60-mph sprints were extremely competitive. Handling was surprisingly composed, comfort was high, and Cobras—those without solid lifters—were quiet. Evidently, middle age has its good points.

Cobra still was a serious muscle car, but it now was confined to Torino Sports-Roof styling in a larger, redesigned body. A 429-cid V-8 was standard, and the new 370-bhp Cobra version could get the optional shaker scoop. A T-handle Hurst-shifted four-speed was standard. Cobra's odd horizontal-readout tachometer was left of the steering wheel. Rear-window slats were a popular option.

Series: Cyclone Spoiler		
Hardtop coupe		
Weight	Price $	Production
4100	4300	1631
Engine		
Type	V-8	
Displacement (ci.)	429	
Bore × stroke	4.36 × 3.59	
Horsepower	370	
Compression ratio	11.30:1	
Fuel feed	Rochester 4-bbl	

Mercury marched lockstep with Ford through much of the muscle age. Sure, it got many of the company's hot engines, but its Cougar never really ran with the wild ponys, and its midsize models were little more than fancy Fairlanes. That changed with the 1970 intro of the marque's best-ever performance car, the Cyclone Spoiler.

Here, finally was a body unique from that of the fastback Fords, a Coke-bottle shape with an individualized flavor. The Spoiler was the pure-performance version of the Cyclone GT, and actually came better equipped for battle than its Ford Torino Cobra cousin. Standard in the Mercury was the 370-bhp ram-air 429-cid V-8, an extra-cost upgrade in the Cobra. A Hurst-stirred four-speed with 3.50:1 Traction-Lok gears completed the drivetrain, while a "competition" handling package and G70x14 tires laced it down. As in the Ford, a Select-Shift automatic was optional, and so was the Drag Pack, which emboldened the 429 with solid lifters, stronger internals, and 375 bhp. The Drag Pack included 3.91:1 or 4.30:1 axles, the latter a Detroit Locker. As with the Torino Cobra, the Boss 429 engine was advertised as an early Cyclone Spoiler option, but few, if any, were installed.

Spoiler didn't use a shaker hood, going instead with an integrated functional scoop. A chin spoiler and rear air foil were standard, and while exterior adornment was left to simple tape stripes, six "Competition" colors (blue, pastel blue, orange, yellow, gold, and green) were available. Mercury went Ford one better on the inside, providing Cyclones with a standard instrument cluster that included a proper round tachometer, and oil pressure, coolant temperate and amp gauges, all angled toward the driver. Torino made do with idiot lights and a weird horizontal-reading tachometer.

Befitting a Mercury, the Cyclone Spoiler was a big car. It shared Torino's wheelbase, but at a rangy 209.9 inches, its body was longer than the Ford's by 3.7 inches. And it weighed about 100 pounds more, similarly equipped. But finally, here was something more than a Fairlane facsimile, here was a real muscle Mercury.

Mercury pulled itself out from under Ford's muscle shadow with the '70 Cyclone Spoiler. It was the same in spirit as the Torino Cobra, but its styling was distinct and its standard engine was the 370-bhp ram-air 429 that cost extra on the Ford. Front and rear spoilers were included as was a functional hood scoop (the shaker wasn't offered). A rim-blow horn, Hurst-shifted four-speed, high-back bucket seats, and a proper round tachometer and ancillary gauges angled toward the driver were standard.

Series: 'Cuda		
Hardtop coupe		
Convertible coupe		
Weight	**Price $**	**Production**
3395	3164	18,880
3480	3433	635
Engine		
Type	V-8	
Displacement (ci.)	440	
	440	
	426	
Bore × stroke	4.32 × 3.75	
	4.32 × 3.75	
	4.25 × 3.75	
Horsepower	375	
	390	
	425	
Compression ratio	10.00:1	
	10.28:1	
	10.28:1	
Fuel feed	Carter 4-bbl	
	three Carter 2-bbl	
	two Carter 4-bbl	

A fully redesigned, third-generation Barracuda appeared for 1970, sitting two inches lower and three inches wider than its 1967–69 forebear. Like Challenger (with which it shared a unibody platform), Barracuda carried on in the ponycar stakes this year, downplaying the previous, dramatic fastback roofline for a regular notchback profile and a hunkier, more aggressive shape.

Barracuda came standard with a modest 225-cid, 145-horsepower inline six and could be upgraded with a pair of 383-cid V-8s, at 290 and 330 hp.

The sportiest Barracuda for 1970 was the 'Cuda. It came standard with the 335-hp version of the 383 and could also be had with 375-horse four-barrel 440; the 390-hp 440 Six Pack; and the crushing 425-horsepower, dual four-barrel 426 Hemi, with new hydraulic lifters.

The 440 and Hemi 'Cudas had beefed-up suspensions, and although neither setup had a rear stabilizer bar, both had five-leaf springs on the right rear, and six-leaf on the left, with thicknesses engineered to equalize tire loads in hole shots. Wheel hop was present, and a careless stoplight dragger could inadvertently light up the tires—F70×14s on 440s, F60×15s on Hemis.

The standard 'Cuda hood had nonfunctional air intakes, but the Hemi came with a functional shaker scoop that was a $97 option on other 'Cudas.

On the street, the 440 Six Pack's vacuum-actuated front and rear carbs came in with little warning, while the Hemi's stiff throttle linkage sometimes snapped all eight barrels open at once. The 440 could keep pace with the Hemi up to 70 mph, but after that, the race-bred Hemi was gone. Sixty came up from rest in 5.6 seconds for the Hemi, and the quarter was handled in 13.4 seconds at 104.6 mph.

Of the 19,500 'Cudas built for 1970, the fabled Hemi was installed in just 666, with just 14 of that number being convertibles.

People inclined to believe that the performance of the 1970 Hemi 'Cuda was a little unholy will feel vindicated in the fact that that fabulous motor was installed in precisely 666 of the year's 19,515 'Cudas. First- and second-generation Barracudas used Chrysler's A-body. With the 1970 redesign, Plymouth switched to the corporate E-body, which made for a longer, hunkier machine. By this time, a fastback was no longer offered, but who cared? With Hemi power, a 'Cuda was the match of most any street machine. Hard to believe that that first Barracuda from 1964 wore a *Valiant* badge. Sadly, the Muscle Car Era was winding down after 1970, so second-year 'Cuda sales plummeted to 6602, a drop-off of some 65 percent.

Series: Road Runner		
Hardtop coupe		
Weight	**Price $**	**Production**
3785	4298	1920
Engine		
Type	V-8	
	V-8	
	Hemi V-8	
Displacement (ci.)	440	
	440	
	426	
Bore × stroke	4.32 × 3.75	
	4.32 × 3.75	
	4.25 × 3.75	
Horsepower	375	
	390	
	425	
Compression ratio	9.70:1	
	10.28:1	
	10.28:1	
Fuel feed	Carter 4-bbl	
	three Holley 2-bbl	
	two Carter 4-bbl	

Aerodynamic testing began to come into its own in automotive design in the late Sixties. Cars of all sorts benefited, but few had the visual drama of the Plymouth Road Runner Superbird.

Like the similar '69 Dodge Charger Daytona, the Superbird was a "homologation special": In order to be eligible to run in NASCAR events in 1970, a given model's production run had to equal half the number of the manufacturer's dealers, or 1000 cars, whichever figure was higher. Ultimately, 1920 Superbirds were made and offered for sale at steep prices that began at $4298.

The metal front-nose clip, with chin spoiler and fiberglass tubs for pop-up headlamps, was fitted to front fenders and a lengthened hood borrowed from the '70 Dodge Coronet. Other aerodynamic parts—including the car's towering aluminum wing—were developed expressly for the Belvedere/Road Runner body, and thus were not related to similar pieces of the Charger Daytona.

Unique, too, of course, were the Warner Bros. Road Runner graphics, which gave this very serious competition car a nice touch of whimsy.

All production Superbirds wore vinyl tops that hid the weld seams left by installation of the flush-mounted back window. As on the Charger Daytona, rearward-facing scoops on the front fenders were nonfunctional on production Superbirds but allowed the fender tops to be cut for tire clearance and suspension travel on competition cars.

Three engines were offered: a 375-horsepower 440 with a single four-barrel carburetor; the 390-horse 440 Six Pack with triple two-barrel carbs; or the 425-horse 426 Hemi, with a 10.25:1 compression ratio.

In competition trim, the Superbird could top 220 mph; at the 1970 Daytona 500, Pete Hamilton beat the field with an average speed of 150. The Superbird went on to take 21 of 38 Grand National events that year.

Although similar at a glance to the '69 Dodge Charger Daytona, the '70 Road Runner Superbird was no competition follow-on, but a unique race machine with exclusive aerodynamic parts—nose clip and rear wing included. The Superbird's finest hour came at the 1970 Daytona 500, when driver Pete Hamilton blasted home at an average speed of nearly 150 mph to take the measure of every Ford (and Dodge, too). Superbirds subsequently took 21 of Chrysler's 38 Grand National wins for the year. Top track speed, at a clear 220 mph, was nothing less than stupendous.

Series: Charger R/T Hemi		
Hardtop coupe		
Weight	**Price $**	**Production**
4000	5800	63
Engine		
Type	V-8	
Displacement (ci.)	426	
Bore × stroke	4.25 × 3.75	
Horsepower	425	
Compression ratio	10.25:1	
Fuel feed	two Carter 4-bbl	

With muscle in retreat, the last thing anyone would have expected to see on the order sheet was the 426 Hemi, but there it was. Granted, not many were delivered for '71, but that didn't mean the Hemi didn't still deliver.

Mopar was holding out better than most against the anti-performance onslaught. Compression ratios were down only fractionally, and horsepower cuts were not severe. The Hemi continued with a 10.25:1 squeeze and retained 425 bhp and 490 lb-ft of torque. Chrysler installed just 356 of the mills for '71, 186 of them in Dodge Challengers and Plymouth 'Cudas.

The balance was spread among the redesigned Plymouth Road Runner and GTX, and the new Dodge Charger and its close cousin, the Charger Super Bee. The '71 Charger was a radical departure from its predecessor, losing two inches of wheelbase and gaining swoopy Coke-bottle contours. It now shared its body with the Super Bee, and though its performance leader retained the R/T designation, the only '71 Charger to come standard with the car's trademark hidden headlamps was the luxury SE version; they were otherwise optional.

But the R/T stayed true to its roots with a daunting underhood lineup. The 370-bhp 440-cid four-barrel Magnum V-8 was standard, with the 385-bhp 440 Six Pack available at extra cost. Topping the roster was the Hemi, which cost $884, not including required extras such as the Sure-Grip diff. A four-speed was standard, TorqueFlite was optional, and Hemi Chargers fed their dual quads with an Air Grabber-type hood scoop activated by a dashboard switch.

A standard blackout hood, faux bodyside air extractors, Rallye wheels, tape stripes, and optional front and rear spoilers made this the most garish Charger ever, particularly when swathed in extra-cost colors like "Hemi Orange" and "Citron Yella." Charger retained this body style through 1974, but would never again have a Hemi. Chrysler dropped the engine from the roster after this year, making 1971 the requiem for this heavyweight.

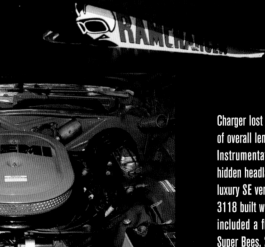

Charger lost an inch of its wheelbase, three inches of overall length, and its handsome styling for '71. Instrumentation and ergonomics improved, but hidden headlamps were now optional on all but the luxury SE version. The R/T returned, and 63 of the 3118 built were ordered with the 426 Hemi, which included a flip-up hood scoop. Of 5054 Charger Super Bees, 22 were Hemis. The legendary engine was dropped after this year.

Series: GTX		
Coupe		
Weight	Price $	Production
4000	3800	135
Engine		
Type	V-8	
Displacement (ci.)	440	
Bore × stroke	4.32 × 3.75	
Horsepower	385	
Compression ratio	10.30:1	
Fuel feed	three Holley 2-bbl	

The GTX was among the precious few 1971 muscle cars that needed no excuses. It was bold, it was bad. Some said it was beautiful.

Once again, the GTX played upscale companion to the budget-muscle Road Runner. Both were part of Chrysler's revamped midsize line (which also included the Dodge Charger), and both got curvaceous new "fuselage" styling on a wheelbase one inch shorter than before. With the new body came a three-inch increase in rear track, which benefited handling, plus a reconfigured interior with a more comfortable driving position and superior ergonomics.

Although Mopar was the slowest of Detroit's Big Three to scale back, not all its V-8s escaped detuning. Road Runner's standard 383-cid four barrel, for instance, lost 35 bhp. GTX engines, however, held out relatively unscathed. Compression ratios were shaved slightly, but the standard 440 four-barrel and the optional triple-two-barrel 440+6 lost only five bhp, to 370 and 385, respectively. The extra-cost and seldom-ordered 426 Hemi held fast at 425 bhp. Four-speeds and TorqueFlites, with axle ratios up to 4.10:1, were still available, as was the Air Grabber hood.

Weight was up by about 170 pounds, however, and quarter-mile times crept higher, by nearly a full second in some tests. The '71 GTX also had the stiffest suspension rates of any Mopar intermediate, and while handling was adequate, most testers concluded that it wasn't good enough to justify the rock-hard ride. But clearly, there was sinew beneath that new skin, and the car could still scale muscle's twin peaks: under 14 seconds and over 100 mph in the quarter-mile.

"All in all," said *Car and Driver*, "we would have to say that the Plymouth GTX is a step forward on a front where all others are retreating. In certain areas, styling and driver comfort, for example, it is vastly improved over the previous model and only in performance, primarily because of increased weight, has it lost ground."

As it turned out, the GTX succumbed sooner rather than later to the forces killing hot cars; 1971 was its last year as a stand-alone model. The more popular Road Runner name lived on until the 1980 model year, but mostly as a muscle car in memory only. The GTX, at least, died with its big-cube boots on.